because he is...

because he is...

meghna gulzar

HarperCollins *Publishers* India

Published in hardback in India by
HarperCollins *Publishers* in 2018
A-75, Sector 57, Noida, Uttar Pradesh 201301, India
www.harpercollins.co.in

2 4 6 8 10 9 7 5 3 1

Copyright © Meghna Gulzar 2018

P-ISBN: 978-93-5277-051-9
E-ISBN: 978-93-5277-052-6

Meghna Gulzar asserts the moral right
to be identified as the author of this work.

The views and opinions expressed in this book are the author's own and the facts are as
reported by her, and the publishers are not in any way liable for the same.

Photographs from the Gulzar family by Sanil B.K., Mehboob Alam, Dhirendra Chawda,
Haresh Daftary, Anand Verma and others. Selected pictures by Govind Singh Sandhu

Meghna's childhood pictures and Raakhee's personal photographs by Gulzar

Additional photographs: Subi Samuel, Shaheen Muhammed, Hitesh Mulani, Raju Shelar

Designed by Sanjeev Kr. Mathpal

Printed and bound at
Thomson Press (India) Ltd

for my dadi
Sujaan Kaur…
whose face we don't know…

contents

papi's word then...

Let me say a few words about the author, after she has said a 'bookful' about me. It's funny – this little chit of a girl – a drop of dew … I ought to be helping her work out her life. Instead, she is working on my life, for a book!

It has been great fun bringing up this girl, 'Bosky'. She has been the core of my entire existence since 13 December 1973, when she was born. I did everything to pamper and spoil her, but her mother was there to keep both of us disciplined! The growing up of a doting father and his growing-up daughter…

I tried to provide her with a boundless childhood, which every child needs from his or her parents, be they poor or rich. It is not wealth or resources which make the difference, but attention, concern and time which one has to provide. I had plenty of time, for I had nothing better to do than what I was doing – raising my child to be a good human being, a creative person and a loving soul.

I indulged all her friends who will find their names in the books that I wrote for Bosky, on every birthday of hers till she was thirteen. It was for all of them. Many of them have grown up at my house and I am happy that they are still around as her friends: Meeta, Zereh, Gulzar and Gudiya…

Bosky learnt to write at a very early age. All children imitate their parents – popping out her lower lip and holding her thinking pen, she would imitate me and scribble on a piece of paper. Chewing an end of her spectacles, she would pose over her book, like me … She started rhyming words, which she learnt in school.

I was going in for a bath one day when she asked me for money, which I refused her. I came out of my bath and there was a letter on my table, properly signed by her:

I have a father,

Who gives me money.

I'd hate him not rather

He loves me as honey.

I love my father too.

He polishes my shoe.

He's sometimes sweet, sometimes funny.

But today I want money,

So away he's running.

Bhawana Somaaya published her first poem when she was only eight. (In the same year, she received her first marriage proposal, which was published in the same magazine.) Luckily for Govind, I did not pay heed to it. And fortunately, I waited till he arrived. Patience always pays, they say…

She honed her other mediums of expression as she grew up, but writing came to her quite easily, or comfortably, I should say. She was in college when her poems got selected for the *Indo-British Anthology of Poems* – I experienced a sense of fulfilment…

Books have always been a passion with me. I can easily spend a few hours in a bookshop. Whenever I went to a bookshop, I always took her with me and let her choose her own storybooks. It was on one such occasion that she pleasantly surprised the shopkeeper and me by asking for a book by the author's name: 'Do you have a storybook of Hans Christian Andersen?'

She was barely nine years old at the time…

We were destined to share many books as she grew older. But I never thought that one day she would be writing a book on me. But here we are! At the outset, I thought it would be difficult to relate my own life to her – I didn't want to impose my own perspectives on her. That would be a very subjective point of view. But how would she know my past, how could she have a point of view on it when she was not even born?

One thing we all fail to realize is that as they are growing up, our children observe and absorb so much about their parents, about us, that their truths about their parents, about us, could shock us…

They know if we don't wash our hands before meals … They know the language we use if we abuse our servants … They know if we are at home and have conveyed a message on the phone saying that we have left … They know we tell lies … They instinctively know our relations with our friends and relatives. They know our hypocrisies…

When Bosky started chatting with me on different issues, I knew that her questions arose because there was so much questionable about me…

I made no pretence. I was honest and truthful and didn't hide anything. I admire her sense of discretion and her own judgement.

In fact, that's what makes a writer…

I know I'm protected
because his arms cradle me.
I know I walk the right path
because his little finger leads me.
He dabbles with celluloid
so I know I can see,
I know I can write
because his ink flows in me.
I know I can
because he believes,
I know I am
because he is …

Meghna

irshaad...

I had taken this picture on the train from New York to Washington ... I've always wondered what Papi was thinking about just then...

The beginning, they say, is a good place to start. And my beginning about my father's life begins at the start of *my* life – since I wasn't an eyewitness to his beginning! It is a daunting task, to try and consolidate a person's life and times into words, especially if you have deep emotional bonds with him.

I have always been in awe of my father – not in the negative sense of the term. Just that, he has always been not just a father to me – but a continuous life experience, a silent pillar of strength and emotional support, a source of inspiration for my creative juices and a legacy that I will always try to live up to.

An objective account is almost impossible when the subject is so dear. Try I will. But if I fall short, what you will get is a very personal and emotional insight into the man the world knows as Gulzar.

Whom I call Papi...

My strongest memory of Papi is waking up to the sounds of his sitar. He's always had a passion for music and the arts. He took up learning to play the sitar when I was about seven and he was in his forties. He always woke up early in the morning (and still does) – before the sun came up! He says defeating the sun is a great way to start the day. Of course, he never disrupted my sleep in this belief. So I would wake up to the sounds of his sitar, as he played in his study, which was adjoining his bedroom. Whenever I stayed with Papi, I slept in his bedroom with him, for the most part of my childhood, even though I had my own room. I remember waking up and going to him. Then I'd rest my head on his knee and fall asleep again, while he played. I'd eventually have to wake up to get ready for school.

He helped me tie my shoelaces while I was still perfecting the art. My uniform had a sash, which he'd knot – he used to make a double knot – in his own artistic and meticulous way. And that trait stayed with me, to make an event of a mundane ritual.

And then there were my plaits! I used to have shoulder-length hair till I was about ten. And every morning I'd be arguing with my ayah, making her do and redo my plaits till the two were at an even height from my ears! I know I wasn't an easy child ... and Papi took that upon him as well. One morning, he decided to resolve the dilemma of the crooked plaits, once and for all! Very patiently, he sectioned my hair into two halves, parting it right down the middle. Then, as instructed by me, he further divided each half into three sections. Keeping the middle section in place, he crossed the right section over, then the left, then the right, and so on. Naturally, he too didn't get both plaits at the same level on the very first go, but he persisted till he got it right.

I now realize the significance of that seemingly ordinary gesture

Many a morning I have woken up to the strains of Papi's sitar.

– he was taking on the so-called traditional duties of a mother, braiding his daughter's hair. And more importantly, he wasn't ashamed of learning how to do so, from his child. He's been a very egalitarian father – never talking down to me, but always talking to me, never instructing, but rather suggesting. And yet, he instilled a sense of discipline and respect in me. It was a very novel way of parenting, according to me. In an interview that we gave together, about our father-daughter relationship, he said something that made it all clear.

He said it was wrong of parents to presume that they know better, or know more than their child does. They may be biologically older than their child, but in their experience as parents, they're of the same age. So if I was his two-year-old daughter, he was my two-year-old father. And we were both learning and evolving together – he as my father and I as his daughter. So he took great pleasure in braiding my hair. He says it reminded him of how his father used to braid *his* hair when he was a young boy...

Above and extreme right: A maternal father! Papi often got me ready for school – tying my sash, even braiding my hair! He taught me how to tie my shoelaces ... and then, a few years later, I showed him how to cross-lace his shoes!

Papi always said that as a father, he was growing along with me. Here on my eighth birthday, he turned eight as a father.

Left: From the top: Papi's brother Lochan, sisters Mahinder and Surjeet, Papi's stepmother – Dadaji's third wife, sister Guddi and brother Bir.

Right: One of the rare photographs of Papi with a turban. Even then, as now, Papi preferred to look away from the camera when being photographed!

The door of Papi's house in Dina ... still standing...

Few people know that 'Gulzar' was actually named Sampooran Singh Kalra at birth. He was born in a Sikh family to Sardar Makhan Singh Kalra and Sujaan Kaur, and as a child, he had long hair in keeping with Sikh tradition. His father, my grandfather, used to braid Papi's hair, as his mother had passed away while he was still an infant. I can't even begin to understand the feeling of not being able to remember what one's mother looks like ... Papi doesn't remember his mother...

There are images of his childhood, deeply etched in his mind – of his village Dina, where he was born, in district Jhelum, now in Pakistan. The narrow lane that led to his house, the large front door of the house itself, the marketplace, and the madrasa Papi and his siblings used to go to.

Someone once sent him a picture of his house from Dina, and wrote that the front door was still the same! But Papi said, the house seemed smaller, the door not as towering as it seemed when he was a little boy. That's one of the reasons he resisted returning to Dina for the longest time – he did not want the memories and the images to become smaller than how he remembered them, when he was a little boy. He wanted to cherish and protected them from the onslaught of time and reality, yet they are vivid in his mind. It was only in 2013 that he actually travelled to Dina – an experience that overwhelmed him. In his own words:

I want to apologize to the people of Dina who were waiting for me, who made splendid arrangements to greet me, who cooked scrumptious food for me and laid out a huge lunch for me. Gripped by nostalgia, I felt very uneasy in the chest. It was not possible to stay there any longer. Dil kuchh is tarah se bhar aaya tha mera ke pet bharne ki gunjaaish nahin thi. (My heart had filled in such a way that there was no space to fill my stomach.)

I couldn't explain my feelings to them. Kahaan jee karta hai phir khaane ka jab dil hi bharaa ho. Bas yeh chaahta tha ke ek lamha mil sake akele baith kar ro sakoon. Lekin woh nahin mil paya. Bas woh namak chhooaa unke haath se – itna hi bahut tha! Woh namak mere apne watan ka tha. Main hamesha apni nazmon mein kehta hoon ke mera desh toh Hindustan hai lekin mera watan Pakistan hai kyun ke woh meri janam bhoomi hai. (How could I eat when my heart was so full. All I wanted was a moment of solitude so I could sit and weep. But I could not get that. I just touched the salt from their hands, that was enough. That salt from my own nation. In my poems I always say, India is my country but Pakistan is my nation because that is where I was born.)

However, he doesn't know what his mother looked like. At that time, the tradition of photographs was probably not prevalent, so he had no visual reference either. Except that once, when he was a little boy, a female relative, who was carrying him in her arms, had pointed to a woman in the marketplace in Dina and said, '*Dekh, aisi lagti thi teri ma.*' (See, that's how your mother looked like.)

Dina, Pakistan, where Papi was born. Local guides often refer to the town as 'the birthplace of Gulzar, the famous writer from India'. *Below*: Papi travelled to Dina in 2013, seventy years after he had left his home.

He remembers that face. The woman revealed a gold-capped tooth when she smiled. And since then, Papi has always imagined his mother to have a golden tooth.

He later asked his older sister, if his mother really did have a golden tooth and she said no. But he still imagines his mother to have a golden tooth that shows when she smiles, like the woman in the marketplace.

The trauma of Partition is the other memory that remains vivid in

Papi's mind. For nearly twenty years after that, he'd still wake up in a cold sweat from the nightmares he'd have about that gruesome tragedy. He was about eleven years old at the time.

Even his date of birth has an interesting anecdote to it – we celebrated his sixtieth birthday on 18 August 1996. But in some records, his year of birth is 1934, and 1936 in others. Some documents even have his date of birth as 5 September 1934. I guess, birthdays being a Western tradition, not too many people kept proper records of them. I'm told that parents used to advance the age of their children for the sake of early admission into schools, so that they would get the benefits of the pension scheme earlier too. But since I'd prefer my young-at-heart Papi to be as young as possible, I will choose to subscribe to his date of birth as 18 August 1936!

At the time of Partition, Papi was eleven years old and living in Delhi. Most of the family had shifted there as Dadaji used to travel between Dina and Delhi on business, and eventually decided to settle down in Delhi. They lived in Sabzi Mandi, a predominantly Muslim area, within which was Basti Panjabia. The ominous signs

Papi completed his matriculation here – Delhi United Christian School, Kashmiri Gate, Delhi.

The house on the first floor was where Papi lived after the family moved to Roshanara Road, Sabzi Mandi, Delhi.

were already blowing in the wind. And as children, Papi, his siblings and his friends used to overhear the elders talking about the precarious situation.

Then they actually witnessed the horrors – corpses strewn on the streets on which they played, rioters and looters wreaking havoc, bodies being set on fire with anything that was found – tables, chairs, beds ... Roshanara Bagh turned into a site of heinous murder, where men would be dragged and then have their heads chopped off and thrown into the nullah there. People they knew from everyday life – ordinary people – had turned into monsters and killers, brandishing swords and knives. My father remembers a man called Samandar Singh dragging another boy, a Muslim, who used to lead their prayers at school. When asked where he was going, Samandar Singh replied in Punjabi, 'To cut him to pieces!' After a while, Papi saw him return with a bloody sword in his hand.

The stench of the half-burnt bodies stuck to the roads which the garbage collectors would have to scrape up with a spade; garbage trucks filled with distorted carcasses; stray limbs left behind on the street. He still remembers those images ... they have shaken him from his sleep for years since then.

Papi always maintains that having witnessed the gory scenes of the Partition riots, he and his siblings would've turned into fanatics, if not for their father.

Dadaji had many Muslim friends and even during the riots, they looked out for each other, saved each other from harm. This spirit of tolerance spared the children – Papi and his siblings – from becoming fanatics. Papi remembers Dadaji saying, '*Pralay aa gayi hai ... nikal jaaegi.*' (Doomsday is upon us ... it will pass.)

On a visit to his primary school in Sabzi Mandi. As a child, Papi used to be very fascinated by the initials of his primary school MBMS – till he realized it simply stood for 'Municipal Board Middle School'!

The nightmarish memories from that time have seeped into Papi's poems, his short stories and his long-standing desire to make a film on the Partition of India. But the prudish attitude of the government and the people themselves, who preferred to keep these scars of history hidden from the conscious mind, came in the way of him realizing that dream. When films like *Garam Hawa* and *Tamas* were made, he did feel relief and consolation. The scars were now being brought into the open – and that led Papi to make *Maachis* in 1996, a film documenting the terrorist movement in Punjab.

But the journey up to there has been long and mostly arduous...

My father came to Bombay on 1 August 1949. After Partition, hordes of relatives had come across from Pakistan and were living with his family in Delhi. Dadaji had remarried after Papi's mother had passed away and had five children from that marriage, besides the three from his first wife, that is, the one before Papi's mother. It was a large family and to add to it, the influx of relatives was becoming a strain on Dadaji. Papi had completed his matriculation from Delhi United Christian

My dadaji Sardar Makhan Singh.

School, and was enrolled in St Stephen's College, Delhi, when it was decided that he go to Bombay and live under the care of his eldest brother, Jasmer Singh Kalra, who had a business in petrochemicals there. Dadaji felt that he wasn't able to look after Papi as well as he would have liked to, and Papi's stepmother was not dependable either. All the children from Dadaji's other wives had brothers or sisters of their own, except Papi, who was his mother's only child. Dadaji feared that he would be neglected – the other children having brothers or sisters of their own would look after each other.

And besides, my father was establishing a reputation of being the 'black sheep' of the family. He had already developed an affinity for literature and poetry, while still in school. There was a distant relative in the family, called Darshan Singh 'Awaara', who was a poet. Though popular among Punjabi readers, he was not very wealthy, and often made his living borrowing from his relatives. Aware of his growing fondness for poetry, Dadaji feared Papi would meet the same fate.

As a schoolboy in Delhi, Papi used to be a keen participant in the '*bait baazi*' or *antaakshari,* as we know it today. He would learn shers by rote to be able to take on his opponent Akbar Rashid who was very good at memorizing poems. Papi wasn't as good and took longer in memorizing them. It was through this process of learning poetry by rote that a deeper understanding of poems stayed behind in him, and from there developed his interest in poetry. Sometimes Papi would cheat – he would add a word to the original line to match the required consonant. For example, he'd recite '*Yeh Zindagi...*' when actually the line was '*Zindagi...*' This was perhaps, the beginning of the poet in him.

By now, Sampooran Singh Kalra had assumed the pen name Gulzar.

Did he always see ...
his destiny in poetry?

naam socha hi na tha, hai ki nahin
'Amaa' kehke bula liya ik ne
'Ai ji' kehke bulaya duje ne
'Abe a' yaar log kehte hain
jo bhi yun jis kisi ke ji aaya
usne vaise hi bas pukaar liya
tumne ik mod par achaanak jab
mujhko 'Gulzar' kehke di aawaaz
ek seepi se khul gaya moti
mujhko ik maani mil gaya jaise
ah, ye naam khoobsurat hai
phir mujhe naam se bulaao toh!

'Self-Portrait': PUKHRAAJ

destiny in a song…

Papi with his dear friend
Jaggi – in the late 1940s.

Papi took the Frontier Mail from Delhi to come to Bombay. Dadaji and Jaggi, a friend of Papi's from Delhi United Christian School, came to see him off at the station. Dadaji advised Papi, '*Raaste mein, train se utarna mat – kahin platform pe ghazlein sunane lag gaya to train chhoot jaaegi!*' (On the way, don't get off the train – or you'll be on the platform, engrossed in reciting ghazals while the train moves on!)

Papi made it safely to Bombay, without missing the train! Mr Burjor, who worked for Jasmer Taayaji, received him at Bombay Central station. What fascinated my father first and foremost about the city, were its double-decker trams, and not the buses. The trams, he was told, were the cheapest mode of transport in the city – you could travel the entire length of the city for just one anna!

Papi joined Khalsa College in Bombay. It didn't offer Urdu as a subject, which was his keen interest, so he was forced to take up mathematics instead, which was considered a viable choice for further career pursuits. (I now know that my aversion to mathematics lies in my genes!) While at Khalsa College, he stayed in Krishna Nivas, in Parel, a central area of Bombay. It was a tenement of single rooms with a common bathroom on each floor. The room belonged to Jasmer Taayaji, who himself lived at the West End Hotel, in downtown Bombay. Along with college, Papi would attend to Taayaji's petrol pump on Reay Road.

Papi was about thirteen years old when he moved to Bombay, to an alien city and an entirely unfamiliar life. I wondered if there was a time when he was overwhelmed by his circumstances? Did the little boy break down and cry?

Still friends half a century later. Jaggi and his wife Shakun on a visit to Bombay around 1991.

Papi says he doesn't remember actually breaking down – 'There were mixed feelings. Subconsciously, the break from the family had already begun. I just felt more displaced, as I was pulled out of St Stephen's College in the middle of the term.' Papi's older sisters were already married while his older brother was settled in Bombay. Papi was the only one who needed to be 'adjusted' within Dadaji's now-remaining family of his present wife and the children they had together. So it was decided that Papi move to Bombay under the care of his older brother, Jasmer Singh.

Papi with his eldest brother Jasmer Singh Kalra and his wife, Rajinder Kaur

On a positive side, Papi says, 'This move allowed me the freedom to manoeuvre myself better ... towards what, I don't know.' This was perhaps something he couldn't do in Delhi, constantly being in the eyes of the family or 'in the eye of the storm', as Papi says humorously.

Papi did feel a sense of emptiness, along with the now-familiar lack of

Dadaji in his younger days.

One of the letters Dadaji wrote to Papi after he left Delhi. Even though he sent Papi away to Bombay, Dadaji's concern and affection for Papi always remained.

belonging. He would wander the streets at night, alone and pensive, mostly around the area of Five Gardens, Matunga, another central area of Bombay, close to Parel where Papi lived. Some nights were spent on the benches of the Five Gardens, while others in some friend's room at the Khalsa College Hostel which he would walk to as well.

Papi says he feels lonelier now, when he thinks of that time in retrospect, than he did then...

The freedom to spend his time as he chose took Papi to the Indian People's Theatre Association (IPTA) and the Progressive Writer's Association (PWA). The PWA would have its meetings at the Red Flag Hall, where poets and literary stalwarts would gather. They had communist leanings, which was fashionable at the time. The young writers would meet at Charni Road, get on to the upper deck of a double-decker tram and travel to Dadar TT, where they would hold their meetings. It was in these gatherings that Papi met and interacted with many senior poets and writers – like Sardar Jafri, Krishan Chander, Kaifi Azmi, Sahir Ludhianvi and Faiz Ahmed Faiz. Books were already a passion with my father who had become a zealous reader of poetry and literature by now. Meeting these authors that he had read and respected gave Papi a tremendous sense of elation. Though there were no conscious influences, these interactions did inspire Papi to work and achieve a place of respect like the literary stalwarts. He wanted to make a presence for himself ... perhaps

Papi's world is made of books. He says they nurture him ... nourish him...

because he was missing a place in his own family, or as Papi says, 'It was more of a denial of the attitude of my family ... that I had no place, and no significance.'

Along with his growing association with the literary world, Papi would also visit painting exhibitions and recitals of Indian classical music. Surprisingly, this attraction to the fine arts was born from within Papi, and not instilled into him by family or peers. He explains, 'It filled the loneliness within me which made me restless. If not for the arts which kept me anchored and helped me channel my emotions, I would have gone completely astray!'

Papi also became a part of the Punjabi Sahitya Sabha, where he struck a friendship with writers Gurvel Singh Pannu, Rajinder Singh Bedi, Sukhbir, actor Balraj Sahni and others. As a part of the Punjabi Sahitya Sabha, they even tried to bring out a literary magazine in Punjabi, called *Chetna*, for a few years, which was edited by S. Swarn.

Interestingly, it was Gurvel Singh Pannu, a Sikh and a staunch communist who had discarded his long hair himself, who cut off Papi's hair. He wore a turban until then.

Papi just after he cut off his hair. Needless to say, it created quite a furore in the family!

It was not a spontaneous decision, but one that had been churning in Papi's mind for a while. He was not a very religious person and maintaining long hair was becoming cumbersome. Also, Papi fancied wearing a hat! He remembers it was the monsoon season and the day after he cut his hair, he bought himself a khaki trench coat and a hat.

Though Taayaji did briefly lecture Papi on the Sikh religion and keeping up family respect and traditions, he dismissed Papi's action as inevitable from someone who was already a 'black sheep'.

Dadaji was hurt when he found out on one of his visits to Bombay. Papi had told him he'd been unwell and hence, cut off his hair. Dadaji had said, '*Rakh lena...*' (Grow them back when you get better.) But they both knew, deep inside, that it was not to be.

After a year in Khalsa College, Papi shifted to National College, Bombay. He was in Intermediate then, the equivalent of Class 12. At the same time, he moved in with Jasmer Taayaji, who had bought a flat in Walkeshwar in downtown Bombay. The pressure of pursuing a 'respectable career' was also mounting on him. To be useful to the family, Papi, in his free time, would attend to Taayaji's paint shop at Lamington Road, a trading area in Bombay. The family wanted him to become a chartered accountant, as they were barely encouraging of his literary leanings.

But the writer in him could not be stifled.

Ironically, even though Papi had friends who were writers and were also involved with films in some way or the other, he was never interested in writing for films. He just wanted to be a poet, an author, and his writings were already being published by this time. Papi wanted so much to be an author that he got a rubber stamp of his name made. He stamped the cover of a book of short stories by Guy de Maupassant, over the original author's name, just to see how it would look – a book with his name as

You have to dream to make dreams come true ... Papi stamped his name on this book of Maupassant's short stories to see how it would look – his name as the author!

the author! Papi still has that book – even though there have been many books written by him that have been published by now.

Papi's involvement in the PWA and IPTA was growing steadily, along with his reputation as a writer to reckon with; and he continued to make some of his most long-lasting friendships there. The Indian National Theatre would have its rehearsals at Bhulabhai Hall. It was at one such rehearsal that Papi met one of his dearest friends – the renowned actor, late Sanjeev Kumar. Papi saw him play an old man – the father in Ibsen's play, *All My Sons*. Sanjeev Kumar was barely twenty-three at the time, but his performance as an old man stayed with Papi. And a few years later, Papi took Sanjeev Kumar, in a similar get-up of an old man, in several of his films like *Parichay*, *Koshish* and *Mausam*.

Another significant meeting was with the famous music director Salil Chowdhury and lyricist Shailendra during a performance of the Bombay Youth Choir.

Sanjeev Kumar probably donned the guise of an old man, more in Papi's films than in any other!

But somewhere on the personal front, Papi was discontented. He felt disoriented, like a pawn, being placed and adjusted into a family instead of naturally belonging to it. Probably, the constant relocating, shifting residences and jobs took its toll, and Papi was unable to appear for his Class 12 Board Exam. After that, his desire to pursue academics diminished and Papi announced the decision to Jasmer Taayaji with a box of laddoos! Expectedly, there was much furore and criticism over his decision to quit studying.

So along with the sense of disorientation, now came a feeling of suffocation within the family, and Papi decided to live on his own. He took up a room in Four Bungalows, then a remote suburb of northern Bombay. Papi also got a job in an automobile garage called Vichare Motors, owned by Mr Sudarshan Bakshi. Mr Bakshi used to visit Taayaji's paint shop, and knew Papi from there. Papi worked on cars that had been damaged in accidents and needed spot paint jobs. Since only small quantities of paint were required, the expertise of getting the exact shade that matched the rest of the car, without much wastage, was crucial. Papi had a natural knack of mixing colours to make new colours. Besides being good at the job, this arrangement suited him fine, as it gave him a sense of independence and, more importantly, plenty of time to pursue his first love – writing and reading.

Papi's favourite spot in his bedroom – his reading chair – and his stacks of books.

Even today, Papi's favourite spots at home and in the office are at his desk and in his armchair, surrounded by piles and piles of books – almost like a fortress around him – keeping him safe, in his very private world of poetry and literature.

But back then, life was still transient. Dadaji was unaware that Papi had moved

Papi (centre) caught up with an old friend from his Delhi days, R. Jhalani (left), who had moved to Bombay. Here, they are on the beach with another friend.

out on his own and whenever he visited Bombay, Papi would stay at Jasmer Taayaji's house and pretend that he was still living there.

Papi worked at the garage for about six to seven years. It was here that he resumed contact with R. Jhalani, who was a friend of his from Delhi. They became pen pals while Papi was still in Delhi and Jhalani had moved to Bombay and joined Bimal Roy Productions. Now that both were in Bombay, they met off and on at Vichare Motors. It was through him that Papi met Debu Sen, who was an assistant to the legendary film-maker late Bimal Roy, at the time. Debu Sen went on to become yet another good friend of Papi's. In fact, it was Debu Sen who took Papi to meet Bimal Roy.

Destiny is written in the strangest of ways ... sometimes in a song!

Shailendra, the original lyricist in *Bandini*, had had a tiff with the music director of the film, S.D. Burman, and they were looking out for a new lyricist. Debu Sen, who was familiar with Papi's writing, insisted he go and meet Bimal Roy. Even Shailendra himself, who knew Papi and his writings from the PWA and IPTA, encouraged him. So one fateful day, Debu Sen took Gulzar, who was still working in Vichare Motors, to meet Bimal Roy as a potential lyricist for his film *Bandini*.

When Papi was introduced to Bimal Roy, his first question to Debu Sen, with Papi standing right there, was: '*Bhodrolok Baishnab kobita ki kore bujhbe?*' (How will the gentleman understand Vaishnav poetry?) Bimal Roy had been misled by Papi's name – Gulzar – and assumed he was a Muslim; so he was curious to know how Papi would write a song in Vaishnav poetry, which is what the film demanded.

Bimal Roy was in for not one, but two surprises!

Debu Sen informed him that 'Gulzar' was actually a Sikh and this was his pen name, and secondly, he could understand and speak Bengali. Bimal Roy blushed in embarrassment, as Papi had understood what he'd said to Debu Sen. But you can't blame Bimal Roy – it is too unfathomable. 'Gulzar' is actually a Sikh whose real name is Sampooran Singh Kalra *and* he understands and speaks Bengali!

Papi's initiation to Bengali happened way back in Delhi, when he was still in school. He used to spend the nights in his father's shop, near which were stalls of books and magazines. The owner would give out books to read at a nominal cost of a few paise, much like the circulating libraries we have today. Papi would mostly take detective thrillers and spy novels by writers like Teerathram Ferozpuri. He was a voracious reader and would read and return the books very fast; so the owner would throw in books that were not very popular with other readers, at a discounted price.

One such book called *The Gardener* was a collection of Tagore's poems, translated into Urdu. Papi remembers that the first poem in it was called 'Maali'. The book's cover had a peculiar design – a sketch of some sort on the top left side of the book, and the title and author's name on the bottom right side. Papi liked the poems for their romantic and Sufi-istic expressions. So much so, that he kept it long enough for the owner to forget that he had it – Papi actually stole the book!

He then began to look out for other books with a similar cover design and thus came across Sharat Chandra Chattopadhyay and Munshi Premchand's works – the same publisher had probably brought out a series on all these writers.

Both Sharat Chandra and Munshi Premchand's stories were mainly emotional family dramas, with stepmothers and stepbrothers and sisters. As a young boy, Papi identified with the stories as they described circumstances much like his own. He was so taken by these authors that his desire to read them in the original language led him to learn Bengali too. Besides, he knew quite a few Bengalis which helped him get familiar with the language.

After he got over the initial embarrassment, Bimal Roy narrated the song situation to Papi. About two weeks later, there was a music sitting with S.D. Burman where Papi first met S.D. Burman's son and Papi's dear friend-to-be, R.D. Burman (who was still in half-pants at the time!) The song Papi wrote was immediately approved and recorded.

'*Mora gora ang lai le*' was created...

Soon after, Shailendra and S.D. Burman resolved their differences and Shailendra was to be the lyricist of *Bandini* once again. Shailendra was hesitant but S.D. Burman was adamant about having him back. Now it was Papi's turn to convince Shailendra that there was no reason for him to feel awkward.

However, Bimal Roy felt bad about shortchanging Papi. He was also aware that Papi wasn't too keen to be a songwriter in films. Papi always found it to be too fragmented a profession – you write a song to fit into a story written by one person, to music composed by another person, that will be sung by a third person, and finally enacted on screen by a fourth person!

Bimal Roy understood Papi's point of view and asked him to join as an assistant director – convincing him that films were a director's medium and he would feel completely involved in the process.

He was insistent that Papi join him, in any capacity – but he wanted Papi out of the 'motor garage' where he worked, saying, 'That's not the place for you!'

In January 1960, Papi joined Bimal Roy Productions as assistant director to his Bimal*da*...

Debu Sen (third from left) was the one who took Papi to meet Bimal Roy. And Papi wrote his first song – '*Mora gora ang lai le...*'

Bimal*da* ... Papi's mentor
and guru.

shaam ke kohre mein behta hua khaamosh nadi ka chehra
gandumi kohre mein jalte hue aankhon ke chirag
ik lagaataar sulagtaa hua sigret ka dhuaan
neend mein doobi hui dur ki maddham aawaaz
ajnabi khwaabon ke udte hue saayon ke taley
mom ki tarah pighalte hue chehre ke nakoosh
har naye khwaab ki dhun sunke badal jaate hain
aisa lagta hai na soyega, na jaagega, na bolega kabhi
shaam ke kohre mein behta hua khaamosh nadi ka chehra

'*Portrait of Bimal Roy*' — PUKHRAAJ

meanderings and musings...

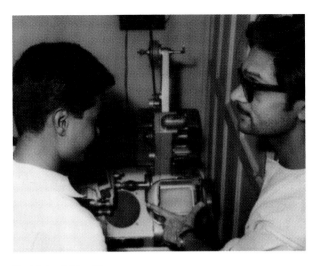

Papi joined Bimal*da* as an assistant in January 1960.

Papi's first film as an assistant to Bimal*da* was *Kaabuliwala*. He also wrote a song for the film. Then came *Prem Patra* for which he wrote one song as well. Papi would also work on scenes with Bimal*da*, because of his leanings as a writer. He was also given an independent script to work on, based on the novel *Amrita Kumbher Sandhane* (*Amrit Kumbh ki Khoj*). This brought Papi in contact with Samaresh Basu, who was the author of the novel, thereby increasing his familiarity with, and thus affinity for, Bengali literature. In fact, years later, Papi made two films based on Samaresh Basu's stories, *Kitaab* and *Namkeen*. Samaresh Basu wrote about the Indian lower-middle class, which he identified with. Coming from the same strata himself, Papi could identify with Samaresh Basu, as well as his writings. In fact, *Kitaab* has echoes of Papi's own childhood in it – the little boy living with his sister and jijaajee (brother-in-law), the way he is treated by them, making him feel obliged instead of wanted in the family, and the little boy running away from home.

However, Papi dismisses the assumption that most of his films were biographical, or reflected the phase of his life at the time, as is generally assumed. Papi avers, 'Any creation, whether in the choice of characters or subject, reveals the creator. The colours, themes and textures of a painting reveal the temperament of the painter. In films, the parallels are more obvious as it is a far more verbose medium with characters, frames, lighting, music and the like.'

The most obvious thread running through all of Papi's films, however, is the exploration of the complexity and fragility of human relationships ... an inclination he developed perhaps during his days with his mentor, Bimal*da*.

Papi remembers his Bimal*da* very fondly. He and his colleagues, Debu Sen, R. Jhalani and Mukul Dutt, used to call Bimal*da* 'married print'. In film terminology, when the picture and sound negatives are fused together, the positive print is called a 'married print'. It was a joke among Bimal*da*'s assistants that he was married to films!

Bimal*da* would work all day, in two shifts – 7 a.m. to 2 p.m. and 2 p.m. to 10 p.m. – and would rarely sit down on the sets. His assistants would vie with each other to give the clap before the shot. The clapboard those days used to be quite broad and sturdy and the clapper could use it as a rest to sit on. It was considered disrespectful of the assistants to sit while Bimal*da* was standing. Such was the awe and regard Papi and his colleagues had for Bimal*da*.

Papi remembers Bimal*da* as being addicted to his work – which meant Papi spent long hours in the sound and editing studios.

Bimal*da* was also addicted to tea and cigarettes and consumed both in large quantities through the day. In fact, if his assistants had to give him some bad news or anticipated a scolding, they would instruct the spot boy to take a cup of tea for Bimal*da* first. A hot cup of tea would actually cool him down!

Bimal*da*'s office was in Mohan Studios, Andheri, in northern Bombay. His film sets were erected there and the studio had its own lab and editing room in the premises itself. One night, after shooting packed up at 10, Bimal*da* instructed Papi to continue working in the editing room and make the soundtracks for a particular sequence that he wanted to see the next day. Papi was also allowed to report for the next day's shoot at 12 noon instead of 7 a.m. since he would be working through most of the night. Bimal*da*'s assistants admired his commitment to his work, but grumbled about the long hours under their breath too. Nevertheless, they did as he said.

So Papi was in the editing room, making soundtracks for the sequence, when at around 2 a.m. the phone rang. It was Bimal*da*. He wanted to know whether Papi had put a certain house-lizard's sound at the required place in the scene. Papi told him he had. Bimal*da* instructed Papi to remove that sound and keep that space blank. He had just recorded the house-lizard's sound, exactly as he wanted it, at home on his Grundig recorder.

'Married print' indeed!

Even his actors were not spared. Bimal*da* would go on extending the shooting shift without telling the actors or the unit. One day, on the sets of *Bandini*, renowned actor, the late Nutan*ji*, who was newly married then, burst into tears in-between shots. She was worried that the constant late pack-ups of the shooting would not go down well with her husband, who was very disciplined and punctual, being from the armed

Papi and Meenaji shared an unusual relationship that was bound by their passion for poetry. Here they are on the sets of Papi's first film, *Mere Apne.*

forces. But out of sheer reverence for Bimal*da,* she quietly continued shooting and never once said a word.

In spite of being obsessed with his work and a hard taskmaster, Papi remembers his Bimal*da* as being an extremely affectionate, caring and patient person.

It seemed like Papi had finally found his calling ... somewhat ... and the lack of a sense of belonging was gradually beginning to wane. Taayaji had married some time earlier (Papi does not remember the year), in Delhi, and the family had 'forgotten' to inform Papi. He only met Bhabhi, as he calls my taayiji, when they returned to Bombay and were staying at the West End hotel.

But what affected Papi the most was Dadaji passing away. It was 1961. The pain of losing his father was compounded by the fact that he couldn't be with him during his final moments, or even immediately after.

This portrait of Meena*ji* by M.R. Achrekar has hung behind Papi's office desk for years...

Papi still grumbles about Taayaji not informing him about Dadaji's death and going away to Delhi without telling him. Mr Samuel Tunius, Dadaji's neighbour in Delhi, sent Papi a telegram and that's how he found out ... three days later. Mr Tunius knew that Papi was working with Bimal Roy and had somehow managed to inform him.

Only Papi knows whether he has or hasn't got over that hurt, but I know the effort that he makes to put it behind him, and the attempt is reconciliation enough.

And finally, the dream came true. Papi's first book, a collection of short stories called *Chauras Raat*, was published in 1963. It was dedicated to Meena*ji*.

Papi's second book followed soon. *Jaanam,* a collection of fifty poems, was published in 1964.

In more ways than one, Papi's time with Bimal*da* was very eventful. He came across many people – some with whom he'd later form creative associations, and some with whom he'd become friends for life...

Legendary actor Meena Kumari was starring in a film called *Benazir* which Bimal*da* had started after *Kaabuliwala*. She too had a passion for poetry, which is what drew her and Papi closer together. They would discuss their poems and writings with each other. She kept diaries of her poems and thoughts, which she would share with Papi.

It was an awkward moment for me, to be discussing this with Papi, as I'm sure it was for him too. But theirs was a deep and emotional association, which cannot be glossed over.

'Meena*ji*,' as Papi calls her, 'was a very sensitive person. She was the legendary tragedienne of the Indian screen – the pain in her expression, in her voice and in her poetry, abstract, yet soulful.' This is perhaps what attracted Papi to her. When there is passion and poetry, romance can't be far behind...

Papi feels that the melancholy of her screen persona and her poetry became a part of her personality and she dwelled in it too.

When she passed away, she willed her diaries to Papi which he still has, along with a portrait of her, done by M.R. Achrekar. For years, I have seen that painting hanging in Papi's office, behind his desk.

Papi's first book was dedicated to Meena*ji* too. *Chauras Raat*, a collection of short stories, was published in 1963 by S. Swarn of Chetna Publications. He also published Papi's second book in 1964 – a collection of fifty poems called *Jaanam*. The poems were primarily romantic, capturing moments that one passes through in everyday life. 'Life is constantly moving, never static. Sometimes it caresses you, sometimes bruises you ... and you want to capture that moment, when life touches you...' muses Papi as he transforms the most mundane moments into poetry.

In the mid–1960s, Papi lived in Four Bungalows, then a remote suburb of northern Bombay, in the outhouse of a bungalow called Coover Lodge. On the ground floor of Coover Lodge, lived writer Krishan Chander, while poet Sahir Ludhianvi lived on the first floor.

At one of the Punjabi Sahitya Sabha meetings, Papi met Bhushan Sabherwal, affectionately called Rahi.

Rahi uncle worked for All India Radio (AIR) in Pune then, and his love for literature and poetry led him to the Punjabi Sahitya

Papi with one of his dearest friends, Bhushan Sabherwal – fondly called Rahi. And we inherited the friendship – Rahi uncle's daughter Shabana, affectionately called Gudiya, and I.

One of my favourite holidays with Papi – my summer vacation of 1985, in Perth, Australia ... we were one *big* happy family!

Sabha. Through Rahi uncle, Papi also got to know Om Segan, another dear friend, who also worked at AIR in Pune. Later, both Rahi and Om Segan joined Air India as flight stewards.

I've known Rahi uncle as Papi's best friend ever since I can remember. His youngest daughter, Shabana, whom we call Gudiya, was my classmate and it was only natural (probably hereditary) that we were 'best friends' in school.

In 1985, on one of his month-long postings to Perth, Australia, Rahi uncle had taken his entire family – his wife, Raj aunty, his oldest daughter Shonali (Gogi), son Vishal, Gudiya, their cousins Nikki and Gautam – and me along with him. We stayed in two cottages in a complex called Kings Lake Village, for a whole month during our summer vacations. Papi too joined us there later and it was one very big, happy family. Knowing Papi's liking for crisp, starched kurtas, Rahi uncle would iron Papi's kurtas himself, spraying them with spray-on starch till they were brittle!

In Perth, Gudiya and I were responsible for hanging the washed clothes on the clothes line to dry, while Papi and Rahi uncle would take turns ironing them.

Papi and Rahi uncle were like two little boys, squabbling, not talking to each other over petty fights and, at times, sleeping over at each other's houses. Once, Rahi uncle stopped speaking to Papi for months because he disapproved of Papi taking tabla lessons! Whenever he slept over at Papi's house, he'd insist on wearing Papi's cotton lungi to sleep in, even though he normally wore silk lungis. They would have arguments over it till he would finally wear Papi's cotton lungi, take it home the next day, launder it, and only then return it.

While with Bimal*da*, Papi had also begun to wear the dhoti-kurta for some time. Most of his friends and colleagues were Bengalis and the influence was probably telling. Hemant Kumar, Tarun Majumdar, Salil Chowdhury, Debu Sen, Mukul Dutt, Basu Bhattacharya and others were a part of Papi's everyday circle now.

Papi recounts writing love letters for Mukul Dutt, who was in love with the late actor Chand Usmani. Mukul*da* would dictate while Papi would write, and he would even admonish Papi for reading the letter as he wrote. 'Don't read it! Just write!' Papi remembers him saying.

Hemant Kumar, or Hemant*da* as Papi called him, was very helpful to Papi and his colleagues after Bimal*da* passed away. Papi was very much affected by Bimal*da*'s death and the news reduced him to tears. It was almost as if Bimal*da* had been delaying his own death while postponing the death of a character in the script of *Amrit Kumbh ki Khoj*. Ironically, Bimal*da* passed away on the day of the *Jog Snan* – 8 January 1965, just like the character

Basu Bhattacharya was a good friend of Papi's. Whenever he came over to our house, he always asked for his favourite drink – milk and soda!

With senior colleague Hrishikesh Mukherjee. Papi has written the dialogues and lyrics for many of Hrishida's memorable films including *Guddi, Namak Haram* and *Anand*.

in the script. Papi has beautifully chronicled the events leading up to that day in his short story 'Bimal Da'.

After him, Hemant Kumar became the shelter to Papi and his colleagues – most of Bimal*da*'s unit. He was a playback singer, music director and a producer himself. He helped everyone get jobs, and got Papi to write songs for his films like *Biwi aur Makaan,* which was being directed by Hrishikesh Mukherjee, *Raahgir* and *Khamoshi.* Hrishi*da* had left Bimal Roy Productions and become an independent director by then. Papi worked with him on many subsequent films like *Baawarchi, Guddi, Namak Haram, Anand* and *Aashirwaad,* which brought him in contact with N.C. Sippy, who was the producer of the film.

Hemant*da* also helped Papi buy a house in North Bombay Housing Society, Juhu, then an upcoming suburb of northern Bombay. Papi was finding it increasingly difficult to live with four other people, in one shack in Jassawala Wadi in Juhu, but didn't have enough money to buy his own place. Hemant*da* collected his remuneration for the various songs he'd written and helped him buy his first house.

Rahi uncle and Om Segan had a house there too. Papi also met singers Jagjit Singh and Bhupender there through Rahi uncle.

It was at Hemant*da*'s house at a sitting for the film *Raahgir,* directed by Tarun Majumdar, for which Papi was writing the songs, that he met *her. She* had accompanied Tarun Majumdar's wife and the leading lady of the film, Sandhya Roy, there.

She was going to be the longest short story of his life...

Surrounded by Bengali influences, Papi wore a dhoti for a short period of time. Here he is with Lata Mangeshkar and Hemant Kumar.

humne dekhi hai un aankhon ki mehekti khushboo
haath se chhooke ise rishton ka ilzaam na do
sirf ehsaas hai ye, rooh se mehsoos karo
pyaar ko pyaar hi rehne do koi naam na do

KHAMOSHI

lights... camera... action!

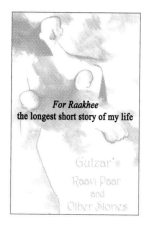

The wordsmith! Papi can express the most poignant of emotions in the simplest of words. This dedication of *Raavi Paar,* his book of short stories, says it all...

'For Raakhee – the longest short story of my life...'

The dedication in Papi's book of short stories *Raavi Paar* probably sums it up best – Raakhee, my Ma, is Papi's longest short story – and is still being written...

Like every story, this one too has its versions.

It was around 1968. Papi remembers having met Ma briefly first in Calcutta and then at Hemant*da*'s house during the course of the film *Raahgir.* Ma, on the other hand, remembers meeting Papi for the first time during a shoot of *Raahgir,* on location in Panvel, on the outskirts of Bombay. The place was Aptegaon, where Ma's farm stands today. She says she bought the land because that's where Papi and she had first met.

Ma had heard about 'Gulzar' – the poet and writer. Her image of him was loosely based on the famous revolutionary poet of Bengal, Kazi Nazrul Islam. She was expecting to see an old man with a snowy beard and says she was thoroughly disappointed when she met Papi – a clean-shaven young man in a white kurta-pyjama!

Ma and Papi met frequently after that.

They had many common acquaintances – Hemant Kumar, Tarun Majumdar and the Mukherjee family.

Ma was very close to Sandhya Roy, whom she affectionately calls Didi. Ma had lived with her for a few years in Calcutta.

By 1968, Ma had already moved to Bombay and was doing work in print ads for products like Lacto Calamine and Hakoba Sarees and singing Bengali jingles on radio. Her marriage to Ajay Biswas was over and she was staying with her friend, actor Chand Usmani.

Mukul Dutt and Chand Usmani had married by then (wonder how much Papi's letter-writing skills had to do with

This is the first picture Papi took of Ma – on the location of *Raahgir*, in Panvel.

Papi is quite a good photographer and would even develop the pictures himself. Some of my best pictures have been taken by him ... as also Ma's.

Ma too would try her hand at Papi's camera – this picture of Papi is taken by her.

that!) and Papi used to come over to their house.

Papi remembers Ma as always being up to some mischief or the other. Gulu, Sarla, Meeta and Khatija were Chand Usmani's friends, who then became part of Ma's friends' circle too, and still are. Papi had a green 1964 model fiat then. The girls would keep eyeing his car whenever he came over. On one such visit, they actually drove off in his car without telling him.

Papi and Ma both agree that there was no one defining moment when they fell in love. It was a slow, gradual process, unspoken and unsaid. Ma says they never had the stereotypical terms of endearment for each other. I do know that amidst family, they call each other Shonu, even today...

They began to meet more frequently – with a little help from Ma's friends. Gulu and Sarla worked at Punjab National Bank and Saturdays would be their day off. They would accompany Ma to Juhu Beach every Saturday evening at 6.30 and Papi would meet them there. The garden near the Parsi Sanatorium at Bandra's seafront, Bandstand, was another meeting place. Papi would wait at the appointed bench and Ma would be escorted there by Gulu aunty every evening at 8.30. Gulu aunty would drop Ma and go to visit one of her girlfriends for a while.

They both fondly remember the many road trips they made together during their so-called courting days. Papi says Ma was, and still is, very fond of travelling, going to new and different places. Ma fondly remembers Papi driving her to all the places she wanted to go to – 'No one had ever taken me anywhere

Ma and Papi – where they first met ... (according to Ma) Panvel, Maharashtra, where her farm stands today.

before, and he was ever ready to travel.' They drove to places like Haji Malang and Wilson Dam, a few hours from Bombay, and would even drive all the way to Taloja (near Thane) just to eat biryani at one of the dhabas there. She admits that it was his sense of humour that attracted her – he was always making her and her friends laugh. Ma says she now realizes it must have been awkward for Papi to be constantly chaperoned by her gang of girlfriends, but he never complained.

Ma and Papi both love to travel and often made long road trips together during their 'courting days'.

Papi says the quality he found most endearing in Ma was her inclination towards the home and family. She would keep doing things to decorate his house at North Bombay Housing Society – buying new curtains, getting a carpenter and building a cabinet here, a shelf there...

Only destiny knows when and why two people come together ... or drift apart...

N.C. Sippy (centre) gave Papi his first break as director and produced several of Papi's films. His son Romu (left) and Papi were good friends too.

Ma and Papi's careers flourished almost simultaneously. In 1969, Ma was signed by Rajshri Films as a leading lady for her first film, *Jeevan Mrityu*, and Papi was being highly acclaimed for his writing in films like *Aashirwaad* and *Khamoshi*.

Around 1970, while Papi was scheduled to script *Anand* and *Guddi,* their producer N.C. Sippy asked Papi whether he had the rights to Bengali film-maker Tapan Sinha's film *Apanjan.*

Sippy saab, as Papi addresses him, had seen the film in Calcutta. Papi informed him that he didn't have the rights to the story but had scripted a Hindi version of the film for Tapan Sinha. Eventually Tapan Sinha had abandoned the idea of remaking it in Hindi. The producer of that film, one Mr R.N. Malhotra, had agreed to give Papi the rights to the story if Papi ever wanted to make it himself. Papi had even worked out another version of the same script for himself – if he ever became a director.

Sippy saab asked Papi for a narration.

Mere Apne – Papi's first film as director. It was also Vinod Khanna's first film as hero. He had debuted as a villain earlier.

During one of Hrishi*da*'s shoots at Mohan Studios, as they were walking towards Sippy saab's car, Papi asked Sippy saab who was going to direct this film. Papi had reworked the script for himself and if Hrishi*da* was going to be directing, it was okay with him. Sippy saab quipped – 'If Hrishi*da* directs the film, don't you want to be its director?' and called him over to his house for a meeting at 4 a.m. the next day.

As Papi finished narrating his script of *Apanjan*, Sippy saab asked him, 'Whom do you see playing the old woman?'

Papi was surprised. Sippy saab declared, 'While I was getting into my car yesterday, I had decided that you were going to be my next director.' Overjoyed, Papi said he had two options in mind – Chhaya Devi, who had enacted the character in the Bengali version, or Meena Kumari.

Sippy saab asked Papi to get his cast together and get ready with the film. A few days later, for reasons best known to him, Sippy saab told Papi that he had backed out of the project, that he had never signed Papi on as a director and had nothing to do with the film! (Well, officially...)

He instructed Papi to maintain that something had transpired between Papi and Romu Sippy, Sippy saab's elder son, and that this project was between them. Papi and Romu Sippy were friends, and Romu's younger brother Raj (Daddoo) Sippy joined Papi as an assistant. Thus, Romu Sippy became the official producer of Papi's first film – *Mere Apne.*

Casting for *Mere Apne* was not easy. Papi had wanted to work with people he was familiar with and whom he had worked with before – actors like Rajesh Khanna, Amitabh Bachchan, etc., but they all politely refused. 'Perhaps they were not too confident of my abilities as a director,' muses Papi. The only one, he says, who was very straight and honest in his refusal was Sanjeev Kumar. He told Papi that this subject belonged to the character of the old woman. 'If you ever have a subject that has a pivotal role for me, I'll do it,' he had said.

Through Sippy saab, Papi approached Vinod Khanna, who had already made a debut as a villain. Vinod Khanna agreed to do the film, as did Shatrughan Sinha. The rest of the cast comprised newcomers fresh from the Film Institute – Danny, Paintal, Dinesh Thakur and Asrani.

By the time the film was nearing completion, Meena*ji* was almost on her deathbed. She was no longer in a position to shoot for the film. As a result, Papi's favourite song in the film, '*Roz akeli aaye, roz akeli jaaye*', could not be picturized and included in the film.

Mere Apne was released in 1971 to both critical and commercial success. It is today hailed as the beginning of the 'angry' films in Hindi cinema. It was also in the same year that Papi got his first Filmfare Award for Best Dialogue in *Anand*.

During the making of *Mere Apne,* well-known actor Jeetendra, who was Papi's neighbour at the time, approached him to do a film. Papi had now moved into Cozihom Society, on Pali Hill, a residential area in Bandra, Bombay. They had been looking for a place in Bandra and Ma had found this flat.

Papi's neighbour and friend, Jeetendra, produced Papi's second film, *Parichay*, based on a Bengali story called '*Rangeen Uttariyo*' (Colourful Chaadar).

With *Parichay*, Papi fulfilled his long-time desire to work with dear friend R.D. Burman.

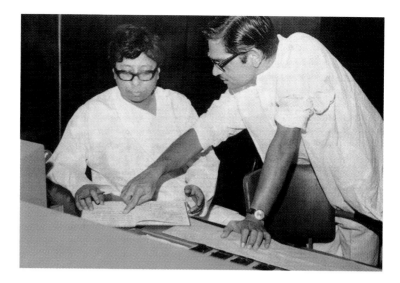

Papi narrated quite a few stories to Jeetendra with not much success. One day he came to Papi saying Ma had narrated a story to him which he absolutely loved, and narrated the same to Papi. Papi reminded Jeetendra that he had, in fact, narrated this story to him and he had rejected it. Jeetendra quipped, 'In that case, you should learn how to narrate stories! Raakhee is so much better at it than you are.'

Ma had read the story '*Rangeen Uttariyo*' (Colourful Chaadar) in a Bengali magazine called *Ulto Rath* and suggested it to Papi. It was apparent that the story had been inspired by the musical, *The Sound of Music*. Hemant*da* helped Papi buy the rights of the story and work began on *Parichay*.

With *Parichay*, Papi fulfilled his long-time desire to work with the musical genius, R.D. Burman. Papi and 'Pancham uncle', as I refer to R.D. Burman, had become good friends since their days as assistants to Bimal*da* and S.D. Burman respectively. They both longed to work together. However, for *Mere Apne*, Salil Chowdhury was the music director as he had a long-standing association with Sippy saab and his films.

Papi's third film, *Koshish*, was inspired from a Japanese film, *The Happiness of Us Alone*, even though *Koshish* was almost antithetical to it in thought. The film had two of Papi's favourites – Sanjeev Kumar and Jaya Bhaduri.

By this time, Ma was also being hailed as an actress of calibre for her performance in films like *Sharmilee*, *27 Down*, *Daag* and *Blackmail*.

Papi too was by then established as a director to reckon with. His films were almost always drawn from literature and were marked for their simplicity and deep understanding of the human psyche and relationships.

His adeptness in exploring human relationships was showcased in his film *Koshish*. It was inspired by the Japanese film *The Happiness of Us Alone* that Papi had seen in the first-ever International Film Festival of India in Bombay in 1952. However, Papi disagreed with the basic premise of that film that handicapped people are better off isolated in a society of their own. He found that thought too reactionary and instead felt that handicapped people should, in fact, be assimilated as normally as possible into mainstream society. He scripted a version of the film, adding the character of the blind man. His script was almost an antithesis to the original film, within the same situation.

N.C. Sippy, who was to produce the film, began to have second thoughts after the script was completed. He suggested that Papi either has a voice-over or subtitles explaining what the deaf and mute characters were saying and doing. Papi disagreed. His contention was that if in spite of having the arts of acting, screenplay, cinematography, music, editing, art direction and costumes at his disposal, he still would not be able to get his thought and idea across to the viewers, he should give up being a film-maker. Sippy saab was so taken by Papi's conviction that he immediately gave Papi a cheque and said, 'If you're so convinced and confident, why should I have any doubts?'

Thus, *Koshish* was made and released in 1972, adding another milestone to Papi's repertoire of films. And Papi had begun his professional association with another close friend from his IPTA days, actor Sanjeev Kumar. From here on, most of Papi's films had Sanjeev Kumar and R.D. Burman, his two anchors – in films and friendship.

Till today, Papi feels that Sippy saab was the best producer he's ever had. He says Sippy saab made films with pure conviction, driven by a singular passion for cinema. He has produced some of the most remarkable films in Hindi cinema. He never interfered with the making of the film once the scripting was over. Papi says Sippy saab was the most spontaneous producer; he would follow through with a whim purely on the strength of his conviction. In fact, Papi doesn't hesitate to go so far as to say that the Hindi film industry has not really given Sippy saab his due.

During the making of *Parichay,* Papi came across yet another short story, this one written by Khwaja Ahmed Abbas in the magazine, *Imprint*. It was titled '*The Thirteenth Victim*'.

Years later, Papi would meet the publisher of *Imprint,* R.V. Pandit, who would later become the producer of his film *Maachis.*

And the world keeps spinning as the circles become smaller!

By 1972, Vinod Khanna had become quite popular. Papi, Vinod Khanna and Romu Sippy had become good friends after *Mere Apne*. They called each other 'MD', to everyone's curiosity. Even today, not many people know what 'MD' stands for.

Papi decided to make a film based on '*The Thirteenth Victim*' with Vinod Khanna. The film was to be *Achaanak*.

Sippy saab liked the story and wanted to buy it. He called Khwaja Ahmed Abbas and found out that he was on his way to the airport to take a flight. Sippy saab took an envelope of cash and drove to the airport immediately. He found Khwaja Ahmed Abbas and handed him the envelope saying he wanted the rights to his story. Mr Abbas was quite taken aback. He assured Sippy saab that he would indeed give him the rights of the story, as soon as he returned from his trip. But Sippy saab insisted he keep the money and that the other formalities would be completed on his return. Such was his drive and passion. Khwaja Ahmed Abbas even went on to write about the incident in *The Screen,* a weekly magazine on the world of entertainment, that never before had a person from the film industry given him money so readily!

Achaanak was a very short script with no song situations. Papi was apprehensive about how Sippy saab would react to this. Fortunately, he was most supportive. He told Papi, '*Ye script bilkul aise hi, phite mein baandh ke mujhe de do … Aur bilkul vaisi hi film banao … Main match karke dekhunga*!' (Tie this script up with a ribbon and give it to me as it is. And make the film exactly like it. I'll match it with the script and see!)

Sippy saab was never daunted by the fact that *Achaanak* was a short film and its length would be a problem in the theatres.

Achaanak was shot in twenty-eight days and had a novel release in 1973: Sippy saab ran a documentary till the interval slot

A film like *Achaanak* could only be possible because of the conviction and enterprise of the producer N.C. Sippy.

of the normal show time and *Achaanak* would run in the post-interval slot. Papi still gleams with pride as he declares, 'Only a producer like Sippy saab could do this!'

Khushboo, Papi's fifth film was based on yet another Sharat Chandra novel, *Pandit Moshay.* However, he just selected the track of the relationship between 'Dr Brindavan' and 'Kusum' and developed it for the film. He did the same thing for his TV serial on the works of Munshi Premchand, selecting the *long* short story of 'Hori' and 'Dhania' from the novel *Godan* instead of adapting the whole novel. Relationships between individuals have always fascinated Papi, along with his deep fondness for the works of Munshi Premchand and Sharat Chandra, since he was a young boy. Papi feels that in spite of Sharat Chandra's stories being set in traditional times, he always respected his female characters. They could have been suffering women, but as an author, he always maintained their dignity and self-respect. This is something that really fascinated and appealed to Papi about Sharat Chandra's female characters and Papi ensured he did the same in his adaptation to film.

When Jeetendra learnt that for *Khushboo* he'd have to were spectacles, he lamented, 'This is too much, yaar!'

Which sometimes left the men complaining. Jeetendra was already uncomfortable about having donned a moustache for *Parichay* and when Papi told him that for *Khushboo* he'd have to wear spectacles too, he lamented, 'This is too much, yaar!'

And with every film that Sanjeev Kumar would do with Papi, he would protest, '*Har baar kehta to hai yeh film meri hai, magar hoti hamesha aurat ki hai*!' (Each time you say this film is mine, but the story is always about the woman!)

The Filmfare Awards of 1973 were extra special – both Ma and Papi won that night. Ma won the Best Supporting Actress award for *Daag*, while Papi won again, Best Dialogue for *Namak Haram*. His collection of the dusky statuettes had begun – he has twenty till date – surpassing his mentor Bimal*da*.

Also in 1973, three star couples from the Hindi film industry got married at the prime of their stardom – Dimple and Rajesh Khanna, Jaya and Amitabh Bachchan, and Raakhee and Gulzar.

The quartet at the Filmfare
Awards – 1973.

main bhi uss hall mein baitha tha

jahan parde pe ik film ke kirdaar

zinda jaaved nazar aate the

unki har baat badi, soch badi, karm bade

unka har ek amal

ek tamseel thi sab dekhne walon ke liye

main adaakaar tha usme

tum adaakaaraa thi

apne mehboob ka jab haath pakad kar tumne

zindagi ek nazar mein bhar ke

uske seene pe bas ik aansu se likh kar de di

kitne sachche the woh kirdaar

jo parde pe the

kitne farzi the woh do, hall mein baithe saaye

'Images': PUKHRAAJ

and then there
were three…

The wedding itself was quite chaotic as they had forgotten to call a pandit! S.D. Burman too participated in the ceremony.

Ma and Papi got married on 18 April 1973. As a child and even now, I love hearing the stories about their wedding. It was a lavish affair at the Turf Club, in downtown Bombay, but it had its share of pandemonium.

Papi fondly remembers how gracious and instrumental Sippy saab was during the wedding. All the groom's rituals took place at his bungalow since Papi's flat was too small. The invitation cards went out from his office and the marriage and reception at the Turf Club were also organized by him.

Papi's shagun from the girl's side too arrived at Sippy saab's house – a baingan (brinjal) the size of a pumpkin! Ma was up to her usual mischievous self – well aware of Papi's strong dislike for brinjals. It has even found repeated mention in his films...

Papi's aversion to the vegetable goes back to the mid-1960s when he was living in Four Bungalows. Having eaten a preparation of brinjals that was not completely cooked, Papi had thrown up. Since then, his repulsion towards them has only grown – 'I like all Bengali things – their literature, their poetry, their music ... even my wife ... everything except the baingan!' he quips!

Ma had overseen most of the wedding decorations herself – with the Bengali alpana (rangoli) motifs everywhere. The haldi and the sangeet took place at Ma's bungalow 'Muktangan' in Santa Cruz, a residential area near Bandra. Legendary ghazal singer Begum Akhtar graciously sang at the sangeet. Ma's parents and

Ma and Papi...
just married...

Legendary singer Begum Akhtar graciously sang at Ma's sangeet.

My maternal grandmother, whom I call Dida, performed Ma's haldi according to Bengali rituals.

brothers had already moved from Calcutta to Bombay by 1971 and were staying with her. Hordes of her relatives came down for the wedding. As did relatives from Papi's side – Jasmer Taayaji, Taayiji, Papi's younger brother and sister, as well as his older sisters were all there at the wedding.

Naturally, almost the entire Bombay film industry turned up to wish the new couple. It was a grand celebration with one minor problem – amidst all the preparations, they had forgotten to call a pandit to perform the ceremony! Finally, a Gujarati pujaari was brought from a nearby temple and he performed the ceremony in Gujarati, which neither Ma nor Papi could understand.

Sunil Dutt, who was like a brother to Ma, performed the rituals of the bride's brother in the ceremony. Twenty-seven years later, Dutt uncle's son, actor Sanjay Dutt, did the same at my wedding.

Ma and Papi went to Kashmir for their honeymoon – and like during their courting days, were accompanied by trusted chaperone Khatija!

When Ma tested positive for her pregnancy test, they were both overjoyed at the prospect of starting a family. However, a very clear line was drawn within the family – I'm told Ma and everyone else wanted a boy. Papi and his driver Pandey were in the minority – they were the only ones who wanted a girl. Ma says even though she wanted a boy, she would keep looking at a print of the *Mona Lisa*, hanging on the wall of her room. And she had developed a sudden liking for baasi (stale) rotis with honey, along with pangs for dahi vadas and paani puri as Papi fondly remembers. He would put on an LP that he had of renowned

Sunil Dutt performed some of the rituals meant for the bride's brother.

sitar maestro Pandit Ravi Shankar and sarod maestro Ali Akbar Khan — he says the music soothed both her and me.

Papi says he vividly remembers a vision of Ma sitting in the sun, knitting and quite pregnant. He says, never before or again, has he seen such a glow on Ma's face. At that moment, he says, he fell in love with Ma all over again...

Twenty-seven years later, Sanjay Dutt graced my wedding the same way. He, along with Goldie Behl, performed the rituals meant for the bride's brother...

Papi remembers his greatest fear being that Ma would end up having her delivery in a car. Renowned film producer and distributor N.N. Sippy had once recounted to Papi how his first child was born in a car, as they couldn't get to the hospital soon enough. This fear stayed with Papi, making him so wary that all of Ma's things were ready and packed much before she needed to go to the hospital.

Ma's first pains started on the night of 12 December 1973 — Papi was sleeping while Ma was up knitting. She mistook the pain for indigestion and took a Digene! Eventually she called Mr and Mrs Gokhale, our family doctors, and all of them went to Elizabeth Nursing Home the next morning, for what they thought was a routine visit. On reaching there, the obstetrician,

This is Papi's favourite picture of Ma – taken by him in Kashmir, while on their honeymoon.

This picture always amuses Papi. Ma and Khatija trying to whistle through almond shells.

Dr Cama, informed them that Ma's water had broken and that Papi would have to go back to get Ma's things.

I was on my way to enter their world!

Ma's delivery date was supposed to be in the first week of January so there was no room available for her in the nursing home. They even had to induce the labour pains to facilitate the delivery. Ma says she kept flitting in and out of consciousness because of the epidurals. She remembers the wait as interminable with not much happening. In one of her bouts of consciousness, she saw the whole family present there and wondered if she was dying.

The next time she came around to consciousness, she was told she had given birth to a baby girl – and she went unconscious right there, again!

I was born on 13 December 1973, at around 3.30 p.m., about two weeks premature. Papi says I made it in time for the 'first show' – referring to the movie timings in theatres. Ma stayed at the nursing home for about eleven days and then came home to her 'maika', which was adorned with flowers to welcome

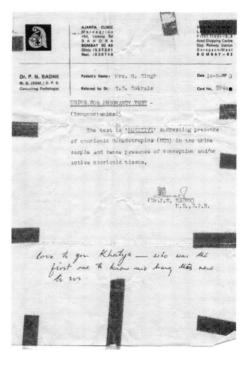

Ma's pregnancy test report. Ma's dear friend Khatija was the first one to know and break the news that Ma was pregnant.

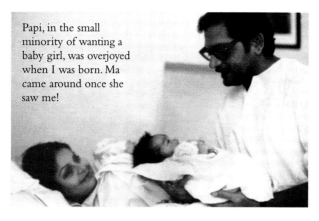

Papi, in the small minority of wanting a baby girl, was overjoyed when I was born. Ma came around once she saw me!

the new mum. Papi named me 'Bosky' after the Chinese silk of the same name. He says I was very soft when I was born. Ma named me 'Meghna' after the river in her birthplace, Bangladesh.

Ma fondly remembers that Papi would pander to her every whim during that time. She wanted to walk on the streets with me in a pram. It was not possible for them to do so in the neighbourhood for fear of being mobbed. So Papi would drive us about an hour away from the city, to a maidaan near the Ahmedabad highway, past Vasai. The pram would be unfolded out of the boot of the car and Ma and Papi would stroll in the maidaan with me in the pram, till she had had enough.

Sometimes I feel like I've witnessed my own childhood – observing it from the outside – the images are so vivid. But I know these are not recollections of my memory. They come from

Ma came home with me to her parents' house. Seen here, my dida, Basanti Majumdar (extreme left) and my dadu, Sachindranath Majumdar (extreme right).

reading the baby book about me that Papi and Ma have so lovingly maintained, right from the report of Ma's pregnancy test to the first-ever article I had written for *The Times of India* when I was in college. Papi still keeps the book up to date with all the major events in my life.

Another treasure that Papi gifted me was the book he wrote each year for my birthday, till I was thirteen. They were published and

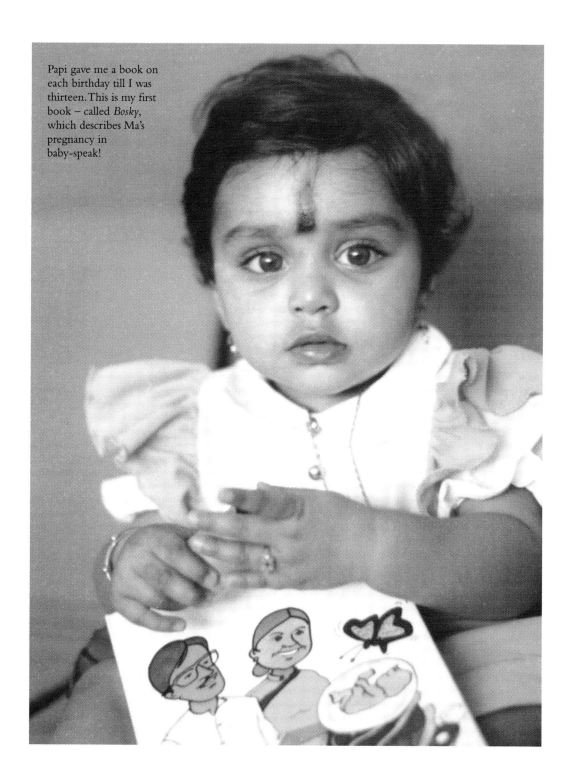

Papi gave me a book on each birthday till I was thirteen. This is my first book – called *Bosky*, which describes Ma's pregnancy in baby-speak!

Famous firsts

First time in the water

First trip to a zoo

First cartoon movie

First shopping trip

First garden

First snowman

First time lost

Other important "firsts"

Papi and Ma have chronicled my life in my baby book – and Papi has kept it pretty up to date!

distributed among my friends, my classmates and at my birthday parties. It fills me with pride to know that not many daughters have this privilege. And that so many other children have grown up reading and enjoying these books.

In a way, Papi has been like a surrogate father to my closest friends – Sonia and Monia when I was younger; and later Meeta, Gulzar (yes, I have a friend called Gulzar too!), Zereh and Gudiya. We have practically grown up together since school and Papi is very proud to say that he's raised *all* of us. Papi has always been warm and welcoming to all my friends – he has made an effort to know each one of them well. So much so that often my friends would come to him with their problems instead of going to their own parents! All of them knew he pampered me, and whenever they came over, they often got pampered too – with presents like chocolates and books. Since Papi and Ma were separated, the absence of a mother in the house who would discipline us meant we were free to make as much mischief as we wanted! I remember using one of Papi's antique vases as a candle mould once. Naturally, it had to be broken for the candle to come out.

From left, Meeta, Gulzar, I and Zereh. We've been friends since school and Papi has pampered us all!

because he is... ❀ 66

Both of them doted on me ... and Ma was the one who had to make sure both Papi and I wouldn't get spoilt!

There was never any fear of a scolding from Papi. He had always encouraged creativity – in any form – in me. So, there was no scolding. In fact, he was quite amused with the attempt.

Papi still has that candle displayed in his study.

Papi's first book for me chronicles Ma's pregnancy. He felt that the excitement of a newborn child often overshadows the experiences that the mother goes through. So he decided to write about Ma's pregnancy and the book was written in 'baby-speak' or *tutli zabaan*, which made it even more enjoyable.

The first poem Papi wrote for me was when I was about four days old:

> *bittoo rani Bosky*
> *boond giri hai os ki*
> *os ka daana moti hai*
> *Bosky jisme soti hai*

By 1974, Papi had already begun work on *Aandhi*. It was being produced by J. Om Prakash who was one of Ma's producers and like a father figure to her. J. Om Prakash was

Still fond of travelling, now I became a part of their many road trips!

An avid traveller, Papi has traversed almost the entire country by road. Here he is with friend and associate Bhooshan Banmali, on one such trip in the hills.

keen to work with Sanjeev Kumar and the eminent Bengali actor Suchitra Sen. The idea appealed to Sanjeev Kumar too. Initially, the film was to be based on a story by writer Sachin Bhowmick. But Papi found it too clichéd and formulaic. He felt, in order to do justice to an unusual combination like Sanjeev Kumar and Suchitra Sen, an unusual story was needed. Fortunately, even Sachin Bhowmick agreed with Papi and the idea of *Aandhi* was decided upon.

At the same time, Papi was working on another film project with the renowned writer Kamleshwar. However, the producer of the film, Mr Mallikarjun Rao, preferred a story that Papi's colleague Bhooshan Banmali had narrated. The story was to become the film *Mausam*. It was decided that Kamleshwar would write the novel of the film instead.

But creative minds can't really be fettered – as Papi was working on the scripts of both *Mausam* and *Aandhi* at about the same time, Kamleshwar would often interact with Papi on both scripts. He eventually ended up writing the novels based on both the films – *Kaali Aandhi* (Dark Storm) based on *Aandhi* and *Aagaami Ateet* (The Coming Past) based on *Mausam*.

Bhooshan uncle and Usha aunty were like family to us and I have many wonderful memories of them.

Papi and Bhooshan Banmali had a long creative association together. Papi had met him much earlier in Delhi, where he edited a magazine titled *Nayi Sadi* which Papi contributed to occasionally. Papi admired Bhooshan uncle's modern outlook to creative writing and they had a common love for the cosmos. One day, Bhooshan uncle landed in

Papi always relishes
the simple pleasures of
life — like chewing on
this *ganna*...

Bombay, having cut off all ties with his life in Delhi. He stayed with Papi for a few days ... then a few more ... and then for a long time, making him the only exception – not too many people have lived with Papi for an extended period of time. Bhooshan uncle worked closely with Papi through many films. Papi loves to travel by road, and he and Bhooshan uncle have made many car journeys together all across the country. My memory of Bhooshan uncle is him teaching me how to play chess and how to swim. He would throw me into the middle of the swimming pool and insist I swim back to the edge myself! His wife, Usha aunty, has spent many an afternoon with me – we would do handicrafts or paint together.

It was noted journalist Bhawana Somaaya, who in the course of her several interviews with Papi, noticed that my paintings were mostly of houses. She has even mentioned it in an interview that was reproduced in her book, *Take 25*. It was probably my subconscious fixation with homes, since I came from a proverbial 'broken home' myself.

And during the course of our many chats for this book, Papi and I discovered that in most of his films, the houses were dilapidated – or there were khandars (ruins). They appeared in films like *Mere Apne, Khushboo, Aandhi, Kinaara* and *Namkeen,* and presumably reflected his transient life. I also pointed out that when the houses weren't dilapidated, and were well done, they always had stone walls – much like the living room of his own house – again visible in *Achaanak, Aandhi, Mausam* and even *Maachis.*

It would be a long time before Papi directed a film based on one of his own original stories, even though he had already written *Guddi* in 1970–71.

Until *Libaas,* which was his original story, most of the films Papi directed were based on stories by other literary writers, although he would adapt the story to suit him and thoroughly work out a detailed screenplay himself. He says he never felt confident enough about himself as a good literary writer.

Aandhi was shot first, around 1974, as J. Om Prakash had suggested, '*Aandhi ke baad Mausam achchha hota hai...*' (After the storm [*Aandhi*], the weather [*Mausam*] gets better.)

Ma accompanied Papi to the outdoor in Kashmir with me in tow. As we returned from Kashmir, paradise got left behind. Papi and Ma went their separate ways.

Speculations are aplenty, as are the reasons. I would like to believe that they are two good people, who were just not good together. And since nobody questioned why they came together, they needn't have to explain why they parted. What transpires between two people should remain just there – between the two people. I was raised to respect their reasons and appreciate the fact that I was spared the emotional scars of squabbling parents and bitter mudslinging.

Ma resumed working in films and that's my silver lining – Indian cinema would otherwise have been deprived of one of its most talented and graceful actresses.

Ma and I accompanied Papi to Kashmir for the outdoor shooting of *Aandhi*. That was our last holiday together ... for the next thirty years or so...

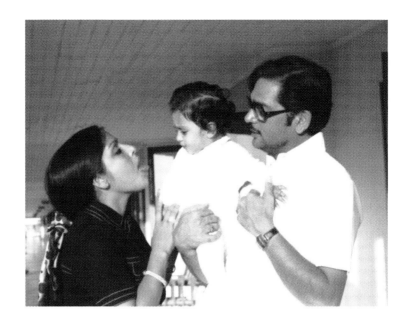

sheher ki bijli gayi
band kamre mein bahot der talak kuchh bhi dikhai na diya
tum gayi thi jis din
us roz bhi aisa hi hua tha
aur bahot der ke baad
aankhen tariki se maanus hui toh
phir se darvaaze ka khaaka sa nazar aaya mujhe

Unpublished

films, fables and friends…

Papi with Sanjeev Kumar (but naturally!) and Suchitra Sen on the sets of *Aandhi*.

Right from their inception, *Aandhi* and *Mausam* have somehow been linked – work on their scripts happened together between Papi, Bhooshan uncle and Kamleshwar.

While *Aandhi* was premiering, Papi was shooting for *Mausam* and during the premiere of *Mausam,* Papi was reshooting portions of *Aandhi*.

Aandhi had been banned during the Emergency of 1975 as the then government felt Suchitra Sen's character, Aarti Devi, mirrored Mrs Indira Gandhi, our prime minister at the time. Papi had to reshoot certain scenes that suggested Aarti Devi smoked and drank occasionally. And a whole new scene was added where Aarti Devi was shown saying in so many words, 'Indira Gandhi is my ideal...', to remove any traces that could make the film seem biographical. However, Papi still maintains that there were hardly any similarities between Suchitra Sen's character and Indira Gandhi, but that Indira Gandhi was the correct model for the character of a female politician.

The film had already run for about twenty or twenty-two weeks when it got banned; so it wasn't a huge setback to the producer, J. Om Prakash. However, he was very keen to make whatever changes necessary and get the film back into the theatres.

Papi was more disappointed only because when the ban was enforced, he was in Moscow for the film festival and *Aandhi* had to be withdrawn from the festival due to the ban.

By the time *Aandhi* was given a clean chit by the censors again, the people had given their verdict to the Congress government and it was on its way out.

I was around two years old when Papi took me along with him to Kashmir for the outdoor shooting of *Mausam*. Kashmir was almost like second home to me as I went there every few months with either Papi or Ma on their respective outdoor shootings.

I wondered if it was cumbersome for him to have an infant around while he was working – to which Papi's reply brought a lump to my throat: 'When something is an intrinsic part of you, how can it ever disturb you?'

I know there were always ayahs, mine as well as those of the other children. Actor Sharmila Tagore had got her son Saif along during *Mausam*'s outdoor, and on Ma's outdoors there would be her co-star and legendary actor Amitabh Bachchan's children, Shweta and Abhishek, along with his wife Jaya aunty; as also film producer Ramesh Behl's children, Nano and Goldie, with their mother, Bubble aunty. Before Switzerland took over, we'd all be camped in Kashmir at least a couple of times a year.

However, Papi says, on the outdoor of *Mausam* it was the mole on his face that helped him babysit me. As a child, I would

Papi had taken me along to Kashmir on the outdoor of *Mausam* where he kept me amused with the mole on his face!

I often had other star children for company on the various outdoor shoots of my parents. Here I am with Shweta (Bachchan) Nanda and Abhishek Bachchan.

be very fascinated with the mole on Papi's right cheek and would try to touch it. Just then, he would make a kind of growling sound and pretend to bite my finger. This game kept me entertained throughout the stay in Kashmir and thus saved Papi from having a cranky baby on his shoot.

The music for *Mausam* was composed by veteran music director Madan Mohan as the producer Mr Mallikarjun Rao had an arrangement with him. In any other circumstances, when he was free to choose, Papi would always have R.D. Burman as his music director.

Papi's relationship with Pancham uncle was anything but formal or professional – yet they had a very fruitful creative association. Papi reminisces that most of their music sittings took place in the most unassuming places – driving around in a car, travelling to places, even in Pancham uncle's kitchen! He was a very good cook and his speciality was pork.

Not many people know that R.D. Burman was very interested in chillies. He had a flourishing chilli garden on the terrace of his garage with chillies of different species and varieties. He would often cross different varieties and develop new breeds of chillies himself. Being an avid cook, he would often ask anyone who went abroad to bring him packets of baby corn, mixtures of soups and sauces as well, which weren't readily available here then. Rahi uncle, who was a flight steward with Air India, often brought these things for him from his trips abroad.

Their first music sitting together took place in Pancham uncle's car. He picked Papi up on his way to Rajkamal Studios in Parel, where he was recording the background music for another film. On the drive, they discussed tunes and words and rhythms – Pancham uncle would beat a rhythm on the dashboard of the car, on the steering wheel, doors and even the bonnet! They reached Rajkamal Studios and Pancham uncle sent Papi off: 'Go back home – or you'll disturb me in my background work!' And Papi left.

It was around midnight when Pancham uncle came and woke Papi up from his sleep. 'Come, let's go for a drive ... *kuchh sunaana hai...*' (Want you to hear something). He had got a tune on an audio cassette, which they heard in his car, driving around the city streets in the middle of the night. Words kept being added or changed, as did the tune. It was dawn when he dropped Papi back home and the song was ready. Papi had been baptized to R.D. Burman's way of working and it became clear to him that this was how it was always going to be. Ironically, the song they made was for *Parichay: 'Musaafir hoon yaaron, na ghar hai na thikaana, mujhe chalte jaana hai...'*

What Papi looked forward to the most was the recording of the background music sessions with Pancham uncle, as during lunchtime, celebrated singer and Pancham uncle's wife, Asha Bhosle (Asha*ji*), would bring lunch

Papi and Pancham uncle were 'in tune' with each other and it reflected in the songs they created together.

This is Papi's favourite picture of R.D. Burman – entangled in wires.

from home, cooked by her. She was an outstanding cook and there would often be cooking competitions between her and Pancham uncle.

It was only on Ashaji's persuasion that the album *Dil Padosi Hai* came into being, as she literally pestered Pancham uncle and Papi into it. Pancham uncle didn't consider a private album to be professional work – like giving music for films. So the sittings for *Dil Padosi Hai* took place at Papi's house – Pancham uncle would finish the day's 'professional' work in his music room and then say, *'Chal, ab faaltu kaam ke liye tere yahan chalte hain…!'* (Come, now let's go to your place for the trivial work!)

And only a musical genius could create a triviality so wonderful!

Pancham uncle's favourite joke, says Papi, was where one man asks another, 'I believe in your country, people say "f" instead of "p"? To which the second man replies, "*Faagal hai kya!*"' It was really not very funny, but Pancham uncle would be very amused every time he narrated it. '*Faagal hai kya!*' also became a catchphrase between them. When Papi took the words of '*Mera kuchh saamaan…*' (from *Ijaazat*) to him, to compose a tune for it, he is believed to have said, '*Faagal hai kya! Kal Times of India le aayega aur kahega is news item pe dhun banaa de!*' (Are you crazy? Tomorrow you'll bring me the *Times of India* and say – compose a tune for this news item!)

The words of '*Mera kuchh saamaan…*' were in free verse with no rhyme!

Papi imitating his favourite picture of Pancham uncle.

Most of Papi's songs with R.D. Burman were created in the most unusual of settings – driving around in their car, travelling, cooking ... *Dil Padosi Hai* was one such non-film album that showcased their creativity.

One afternoon, Papi was over at Pancham uncle's place, who was cooking and listening to an LP he had. The song had a particular phrase, which was somewhat repetitive, in a circular sort of way. Pancham uncle was very fascinated by that phrase and kept playing that bit over and over. He asked Papi to put some words to the tune. He extended the phrase by adding a few notes himself and composed another phrase for its culmination. Papi kept filling in the tune with his words. Pancham uncle asked him to use it in *Ijaazat* but there was no place for another song in the film. This newly 'cooked' song was then used in the title sequence of *Ijaazat*. '*Chhoti si kahani se, baarishon ke paani se, saari vaadi bhar gayi...*' were the words on the circular phrase to which R.D. Burman added a musical phrase in his inimitable style, to which the words were: '*Na jaane kyun dil bhar gaya ... na jaane kyun aankh bhar gayi...*'

Ijaazat was the last released work of Papi and Pancham uncle, as by the time Papi started work on *Maachis*, his next film, Pancham

Papi and Sanjeev Kumar,
Hari bhai as Papi used to
call him, in Moscow.

uncle and his music were no more. When Papi was working with noted singer and music composer Hridaynath Mangeshkar for the music of *Lekin,* Pancham uncle used to tease him, '*Karo, karo … Bal bachchon ke saath kaam karo.*' Hridaynath Mangeshkar is affectionately called 'Bal', meaning 'little brother', by his sisters – including illustrious singer Lata Mangeshkar, who was also the producer of *Lekin.*

Pancham uncle used to tell Papi, 'Whenever I compose a tune, the singer's face automatically appears before me – whether Lata*ji* will sing that song, or Kishore Kumar or Mohammed Rafi. Sometimes when I compose a tune, your "*thobda*" (slang for face) appears before me. That's when I know I have to keep this tune aside, because you will use it in your film.'

Papi treasures this compliment, even today.

Papi has since worked with other music directors. But no one can replace Pancham uncle, he says. 'He is a part of my system. We grew together … and the growth was mutual. Missing him is a part of my system … missing him and Sanjeev.'

Sanjeev Kumar, or Hari bhai as Papi refers to him, was Papi's other dear friend and anchor. They have had a close friendship and a long creative association, which began during their IPTA, Indian National Theatre and PWA days.

After *Mere Apne,* which Sanjeev Kumar refused with utmost grace and honesty, Papi first worked with him in *Koshish.* From then on, whenever Papi's script had a character that suited Sanjeev Kumar, neither of them had the liberty of another option!

Papi recalls with much amusement how Sanjeev Kumar would get thrown out of every film that he did with Papi, at least once – he was invariably late coming to the sets, and Papi is punctuality personified.

Once during the shoot of *Mausam* in Bombay, Sanjeev Kumar came to Papi and said, 'I know you're going to throw me

Two of Papi's oldest and closest friends – Rahi and Kuldip, photographed by Papi in front of William Shakespeare's house in England.

out of this film too ... at least once. Can you do it today? And will it mean that your shoot for the day will be cancelled?' Papi was puzzled by this question. Sanjeev Kumar reiterated, 'But you must cancel the day's shooting. Not that you throw me out and continue shooting!'

When Papi insisted on knowing what the matter was, Sanjeev Kumar revealed that he and Sharmila Tagore had made a plan to see a particular film that was running in one of the theatres in the city. It was the last day of the film in the theatre and the only way they could go and see it was if Papi cancelled the day's shoot! The conspiracy had been hatched in their make-up rooms and Papi was left with very little choice. He let them off for the day and shot other portions of the film that day.

Apart from R.D. Burman, Sanjeev Kumar was Papi's other anchor ... in films and friendship...

There was one condition that Sanjeev Kumar laid down, which had to be met, whenever they worked together – Papi had to ensure that the last day of the film's shooting had a scene with Sanjeev Kumar in it. He would get very emotional whenever his work in the film ended, and thus wanted to be around on the last day of the shooting of the film. After pack-up, he would want to come over to Papi's for a drink and watch *Dumbo,* the Walt Disney cartoon about an elephant with big ears! This became a tradition to be followed at the completion of the shoot of each film they did together. And Sanjeev Kumar would cry, each time he saw *Dumbo,* and every time!

Sanjeev Kumar drank only Black Label whiskey, which was not readily available in India then. It had to be acquired from people who sold it illegally or brought in by someone returning from abroad. He would tell Papi, 'Always keep a bottle of Black Label in your house for me. If you can't afford it, I'll bring one and keep it here, but *you* don't drink out of it!' Once again, Rahi uncle was the one who brought the Black Label for Papi from his flights abroad.

As Sanjeev Kumar's house was strictly vegetarian, he would love to come over to Papi's to eat non-vegetarian food – especially paaya (goat's hooves). Papi remembers one time when Rahi uncle flew to Delhi especially to get paaya cooked and bring it back for them.

Sanjeev Kumar's house was opposite my school, A.F. Petit Girls High School, in Pali Hill. At the end of school one day, as I was getting into the car, I noticed a stream of cars and people around his house. My driver, Sunder, told me that Sanjeev Kumar had passed away. When I reached home, the first thing I did was ask Papi, 'Do you know Sanjeev Kumar has passed away?' I can still picture the look of complete shock on Papi's face as I blurted these words – the news hadn't reached him yet. Papi rushed out of the house the next moment. I was barely eleven years old and perhaps a tad tactless in breaking the news so abruptly to him. With time, I have realized the jolt Papi must have faced, as also the depth of the friendship he shared with Hari bhai.

It was a warm circle of friends with an eclectic combination of people – some from films, some not; but all sharing a common love for the arts – music, literature and poetry.

When *'Mera kuchh saamaan...'* was first recorded for *Ijaazat,* Papi carried it on a tape with him to Perth on our holiday there with Rahi uncle and his entire family. Papi remembers Rahi uncle playing the song over and over again through the day. And at night, he would dim the lights of the porch and hear it while they had their drinks!

Rahi uncle would say to Papi, 'If Bosky and Gudiya (his daughter) get lost, I know they'll find their way back; but if you get lost, God help you!'

Papi is always wary about travelling abroad alone, '*Angrezi bolni padti hai!*' he says. (I have to speak English!)

Papi's first trip overseas was in 1969, to London for the shoot of *Udham Singh,* a film based on the life of Udham Singh. It was being produced by Balraj Tah and directed by Hrishikesh Mukherjee. It was originally supposed to be scripted by Utpal Dutt, which didn't happen, and at the last moment, Papi was asked to go along to the outdoor and write simultaneously as they shot. Hrishi*da* suffered an attack of gout there and Papi helped out in the shooting too, as his assistant. There, Hrishi*da* promised that Papi would direct one of the next two films for which he was working on the scripts. These were *Anand* and *Guddi.* However, Hrishi*da* eventually directed both the films himself and ironically opted out of *Udham Singh* too. The film was completed by Balraj Tah himself and released as *Jallianwala Bagh.*

Papi in London for the shooting of *Udham Singh* – Papi's first overseas trip. He chose to play the cameo of 'Sunil' because the character wore an overcoat and it was cold in London!

However, during the London outdoor, all the Hindi-speaking crew members were to act in the film as well. Papi chose to play a character called 'Sunil', who is a journalist and has to give a speech in Hyde Park. Papi's only motivation was that Sunil's character wore an overcoat and it was very cold in London! More interesting than Papi's cameo in the film was Papi's unexpected tryst with his childhood, through a man called Kuldip Senghera. Papi wrote out the incident, which I am reproducing here.

That was my first visit abroad. 1969.

Hrishida was to shoot for a film based on the life of Udham Singh, an Indian revolutionary, who killed Michael O'Dwyer, the man responsible for giving orders to shoot in Jallianwala Bagh, as governor of Punjab. The orders were carried out by General Dyer, with a vengeance. It happened on 13th of April in 1919. Udham Singh took his revenge in 1940. I don't remember the month. That was probably the longest hunt for revenge. The producer was Balraj Tah, a good Punjabi and a staunch Indian. With these charged 'bhavnas', we landed at Heathrow airport and proceeded to Coventry, where Balraj Tah and his partner friends lived. That was my first journey on a foreign land. A long drive on Motorway-1. The experiences and the events were enriching in many ways. But the incident that enriched me with a leftover, life-long friend, happened at Saxon, while shooting at Saxon Bar. We had not prepared any script in India. Only a few stray thoughts were there in Hrishida's mind. Hence my need there. Balraj had to collect a few Indians every day as per the requirement of every day's sequence. I must say, his friends obliged him in every way. Thus, we over-felt at home.

During a shooting break, we were sitting outside near the Water-Mill with a mug of beer (there, I learnt to call it Bitter), and a friend of Balraj and I got talking. We migrated from English to Hindi to Punjabi. He asked me where I lived in India.

'Dilli,' I said.

'Where in Dilli?'

'Purani Dilli, Sabzi Mandi. Are you familiar with Delhi?'

'Well, I know Sabzi Mandi!' His eyes revealed a glint. I thought he had a great sense of humour. 'Where did you live in Delhi, since I know you have come from Bombay?' He sounded intelligent too.

'Ghanta Ghar!'

'Where at Ghanta Ghar?' he persisted.

Balraj thought we were drunk.

'Tell me why do you want to know such details?'

He was prompt.

'I want to be sure you are telling me your own address and not mine.'

Now it was my turn.

'Where did you live in Dilli?'

'Purani Dilli!'

'Where in Purani Dilli?'

'Sabzi Mandi!'

'Where in Sabzi Mandi?'

'Ghanta Ghar!' pat came the reply. He was smiling. I paused and looked at Balraj. He too was smiling. He was sure we were drunk. I resumed the conversation.

'Where exactly did you live at Ghanta Ghar?'

'Right opposite.' He was serious.

'But that's where I lived, at the right side corner. On Roshanara Road.' He paused this time. Then softly he smiled. Probably he had placed me, or himself. He added: 'Now, it's not a joke; but I too lived *there only, at the corner of Roshanara Road. I realize now, Ghanta Ghar had an opposite side also. That's where I lived.'*

'But there was no house on the other side. There was only a "taal", for selling charcoal and the burn-wood, belonging to one Sardar Arjun Singh,' I recollected.

His face changed. His eye glistened. Suddenly they became very soft. He asked, 'Did you know Sardar Arjun Singh?'

'Of course! I still remember his face and loosely tied turban and the beard.'

His smile was very gentle.

'That's my father. I am Kuldip. I must have been very small then, so I do not expect you to recognize me. Neither do I. But I can place you now. Opposite the Ghanta Ghar lived Sardar Makhan Singh and his family. His two elder sons had migrated to Bombay. You must be the younger one, who had joined films. Guddi and Bir had told me.'

He named my youngest sister and brother.

We were quiet for a pause. We refilled our mugs.

Suddenly he asked me, 'Would you like to meet Sardar Arjun Singh?'

I was quiet perhaps so he added of his own, 'Come, let's go to Birmingham. We live there. My mother, my sister Tosh, my brother Ravi and of course my father. I was touched that you remembered him by his name.'

He took me home that evening, and I met Sardar Arjun Singh.

I bowed down to touch my childhood in his feet and placed my head on his knees.

That's my childhood friend Kuldip, whom I had never met in childhood.

I found him only after growing up.

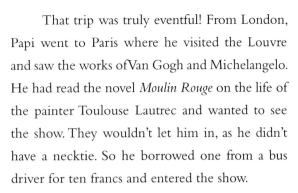

Papi rediscovered his old friend Kuldip Senghera while in London for *Udham Singh*. They used to be neighbours in Sabzi Mandi!

That trip was truly eventful! From London, Papi went to Paris where he visited the Louvre and saw the works of Van Gogh and Michelangelo. He had read the novel *Moulin Rouge* on the life of the painter Toulouse Lautrec and wanted to see the show. They wouldn't let him in, as he didn't have a necktie. So he borrowed one from a bus driver for ten francs and entered the show.

From Paris, Papi went to Rome where he visited the Sistine Chapel and saw Michelangelo's works up close. Since then, he has been Papi's favourite artist. Papi has even written a short story on him, which features in *Raavi Paar* and is now included in the English syllabus of ICSE students.

The Pieta remains Papi's favourite work of art till today. He is fascinated by the image of a grown man (Jesus) lying childlike in his mother's arms. Papi was also very impressed with the detailing in Michelangelo's work — the folds of the robes and sheets, even the nerves and veins that have been meticulously carved in marble. Back then, Papi had no idea that *The Pieta* was such a valued work of art and felt tremendously reassured of his aesthetic preferences once he knew. One can find many reproductions of it, pictures as well as miniatures, around his house.

From Rome, Papi went to Cairo and saw the Sphinx, the Pyramids, the tombs of King Tutankhamen and others, as well the mummies. These were places he had read about, being the avid reader that he was. And when he saw them up close, it was like visiting the history that he'd read. Later, he even travelled to Bukhara and Samarkand, having read about Babar and Chenghiz Khan. For him, it was like revisiting the landscapes that he had read about, thereby reassuring his studies.

The Pieta – Papi's favourite work of art, photographed by Govind.

Right to left: Bir chacha, his daughter Shaboo, Papi, I and Govind during Bir chacha's visit to Bombay.

Papi's desire to enrich himself with history, art and culture, which he calls his khaad – his fertilizer – that helps him grow as a person, will always be a part of his personality. He believes you're never too old to learn – he learnt the sitar in his forties and took lessons in tennis when he was fifty.

But he'd still rather not travel abroad alone. That's why most of his foreign trips would be tied up with either Rahi uncle or Kuldip uncle, who lives in Coventry, England. Or he would simply go and deposit himself with his younger brothers – Shoti chacha in Washington, USA, and Bir chacha in Toronto, Canada.

Papi has three sisters too – Mahinder Kaur, Surjeet Kaur (who is now no more), and Ravinder Kaur, who is called Guddi. When I was around five, Guddi bua, her husband Channi uncle, and children Anu and Riku, lived with us for a few years – Papi felt that having a family around would reduce any sense of isolation that could develop in me.

Jaya Bachchan who Papi calls 'Baba', is another one of Papi's laadli sisters.

Papi has another sister – with no blood relation – who is very dear to me. I call her Uttama Didi. It has been a few years since I've met her. But I do remember the warmth and love with

Papi began the tradition of taking me to visit my cousins at least once every few years during my summer vacations. Here we are in Washington – Shoti chacha, Govind, Manju chachi, Sheena and I.

which she'd meet me, whenever she came down to Bombay. And on Raksha Bandhan, she never forgets to send him a rakhi.

The other sister who never forgets to tie a rakhi to Papi or send it over is acclaimed actor Jaya Bachchan.

Papi did not want me to grow up feeling a sense of loneliness and a lack of siblings; so he ensured that I got to know my cousins – Shoti chacha's children Lou (Guloo) and Sheena; and Bir chacha's daughters Deena and Shabeena. We are all around the same age and have spent some wonderful summer vacations together. Thanks to Papi's foresight and effort, we are in close touch in spite of being across the seas.

It is probably Papi's lack of a sense of family in his own life that made him extra careful about providing me with a positive domestic environment. My mother's house was brimming with her parents, her brothers and their families, while Papi lived alone. So he has always made the effort to keep me connected with my

Papi with his brother Shoti who lives in Washington, USA. They both have the family smile!

cousins. And, more importantly, both Papi and Ma have ensured that I never feel my home was a broken one, but that I had two homes. There was no issue of custody – they let me decide whom I wanted to live with and when. I would spend some days with Papi, then go and live with Ma for a few days. Each was both, a mother and a father to me, sharing me unselfishly. And I have grown up having two sets of parents instead of one...

Papi's sister Guddi (extreme right) lived with us for a few years around the mid-'70s, along with her family – husband Channi (behind), son Riku (sitting in front) and daughter Anu (second from left).

Papi's other brother Bir (centre) who lives in Toronto and Jasmer Singh. The three brothers came together in February 2003 after over ten years!

kai pinjron ka qaidi hoon

kai pinjron mein basta hoon

mujhe bhaata hai qaiden kaatna

aur apni marzi se

chunav karte rehna

apne pinjron ka

meyaaden tai nahin karta main rishton ki

aseeri dhoondta hoon main

aseeri achchhi lagti hai

Unpublished

I am, because he is…

This chapter will probably read as a guide to parenting, but I feel compelled to share this, as it not only reveals a very intimate and sensitive facet of Papi's personality, but could also be very enlightening for parents, single or otherwise.

I have always believed that parenting is instinctive – you don't necessarily need to have good parents to *be* a good parent. And Papi bringing me up the way he did is all the proof I need. He never really experienced a familial environment, having lived on his own from a very young age. Yet, he built a sense of family and belonging around me, in every way he could, nurturing me as both mother and father. Single parenting can be a daunting task, especially when you have a very demanding profession like films, but I never felt Papi's absence in my life. He centred his life and his work on me. While I lived with him, he was always there to drop me to school in the mornings (after tying my plaits and my sash) and would be there to pick me up as well. Since my school ended at 4 p.m., he too ended his workday at the same time.

Papi raised me to be independent and confident of the choices I made very early on. Even the nursery school that I went to was of my choice. He had already spoken to the few schools in the area about my admission. On the appointed day, he took me on a round of the nurseries he had spoken to. The first one we went to was probably affiliated to some convent school; the strict nuns overwhelmed me and I burst into tears. That was not going to be *my* nursery! After making the rounds of a few more playschools, we reached Happy Hours Nursery in Khar. It was a cosy two-storeyed bungalow with a small compound and I was immediately taken by the cheery, colourful environment and the swings and slides in the yard. I didn't even realize when Papi had stopped holding my hand. That was enough for him to

The phrase 'dancing on his head' doesn't get more literal than this! On my eighth birthday.

seek my admission there. As it turned out, legendary actor Pran saab's daughter taught there too, whom I fondly remember as Pinky teacher.

I have sometimes worn the most hideous of dresses only because Papi let me choose them, buy them and wear them, till I grew out of them myself. He believes that all children need to go through their phases of gaudy colours. So when I was barely four and fixated on a particular colour of a car – it was named 'Golden Rock' – he bought a Fiat in that colour, a very loud gold. Even though his colour of preference was and always is white, he wanted to instill a sense of ownership in me – that it was *really* my car, in my chosen colour.

Instead of having to scold me for scribbling on the walls when I'd just learnt to wield a pen, he had a blackboard installed on one wall in my room, at my height, and a pinboard on the other. And I was free to scribble away. The only area out of bounds was his canvas while he was painting. Papi is quite an artist and has a penchant for painting trees. Birds are his other favourite.

Papi loves to photograph birds in flight. This was taken in Kashmir.

He loves to photograph birds in flight and they often make an appearance in the songs of his films too.

To keep me from meddling with his paintings, he got me a canvas of my own, complete with my own oil-painting kit and easel too. And he would shower me with praises for paintings I now shudder to see.

In a moment of teenage revelry, I spray-painted my name across my pinboard and the ceiling of my room, not sparing the fan even – and he let it remain – didn't even reprimand me for it. The ceiling and fan were cleaned up only a few years ago when a refined sense came to me with age. My blackboard and spray-painted pinboard remain though. He has preserved them as testimony of my childhood, along with my dolls, my paintings, videos of concerts in school and holidays abroad, more photographs than I can even count, and letters I wrote to him.

Papi had encouraged a very forthright relationship between him and me – he was my father and my friend – I could tell him anything, ask him anything.

And I had a lot of questions: *Why aren't Ma and he living together like the parents of my friends do? If they both say sorry to each other, won't they make up?*

I'd ask him through my letters, and he would patiently answer all my questions in a very mature and dignified manner – he would never try to oversimplify things because I was a child, nor would he ever speak ill of Ma to make his case.

There are letters I've written to him when he was away, or I was out of town, and notes I've scribbled to tell him I'm taking his car.

He's preserved every one of them.

And this habit has passed on to me too. I have preserved all the letters he's written to me wherever I was at the crossroads

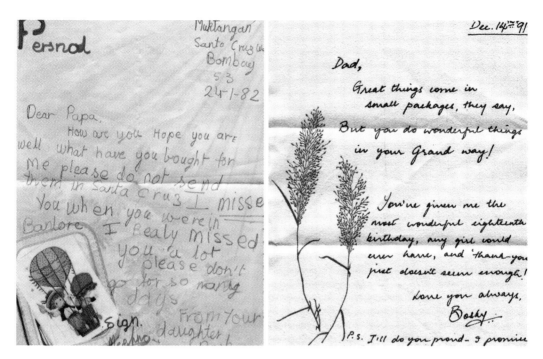

Persnal

Muktangan
Santa Cruz (w)
Bombay
53
24-1-82

Dear Papa,
How are you Hope you are
well what have you bought for
Me please do not send
them in Santa Cruz I misse
You when you were in
Banlore I Realy missed
you a lot please don't
go for so many
days.
Sign. From Your
loving daughter

Dec. 14th '91

Dad,
Great things come in
small packages, they say,
But you do wonderful things
in your Grand way!

You've given me the
most wonderful eighteenth
birthday, any girl could
ever have, and 'thank-you'
just doesn't seem enough!
Love you always,
Bobby

P.S. I'll do you proud – I promise

The writing may not be too good, but between the lines, it all becomes clear...

in life – be it nurturing my broken heart or advising me as I prepared to go abroad to study. Every book that he wrote for my birthday also began with a letter talking about the particular age I was entering, about its enchantments and its pitfalls.

And in his vast collection of books, he has carefully collected all my fairy-tale books.

Cinderella was my favourite story as a child – and remains still. I would insist he read it to me every night. And each time he travelled, he brought back a new version of the storybook for me. Papi's love for books is apparent to the world. But few know that he loves to explore the bookshops at airports while waiting for his flight. He even goes to the airport much before the stipulated reporting time to do so. As a result, I have approximately fifteen different versions and publications of Cinderella.

Papi has indulged me completely, though I'd like to believe I'm not a brat! And Papi agrees! He has to ... he's hugely biased

23/7-94

My Graduate Girl —

You have already broken The record of your father's qualification. Congratulations. You are on a plateau now. You can look at all the horizons and beyond them from here. It needs one more jump to climb into your own personality. You have to choose the direction. Just two/three years more of education. The academic part is over. What ever you do now will be of your own interest and choice. But — without effort one doesn't find even oneself. Make one more effort to find yourself. You are capable of great achievements, that I know. You have only to decide it and you'll do it!

91-A, COZIHOM SOCIETY 251 PALI HILL BANDRA BOMBAY - 400 050 TEL OFF 6461957 RESI - 6498351 6481365
FAX : 604 0477

Papi wrote this just after I had completed my graduation in 1994.

towards me. Ma has been more of the disciplinarian to me. (And consequently to him to!) I can barely remember a couple of times that Papi has raised his voice at me.

One incident, in particular, comes to mind.

I had begun to learn the piano when I was about nine. I had tried to learn the sitar earlier as Papi was keen I should, but the strings would cut my fingers. That ended my stint with the sitar. My music teacher from school, Ms Jennifer Donald, née Pereira suggested to Papi that I take up the piano, as I was quite musically inclined. That particular year, I was learning ballet and karate in school as well, and between these three extracurricular activities, I was left with very little time to do ordinary things other children did – like go out and play. One evening I decided to revolt and refused to sit for piano practice. Papi, in a very stern voice that he has rarely used with me, made me sit before the piano and said, 'Sit down here and play the piece till you get it right … no matter how long it takes.' I was both bewildered and fearful, and burst into a wail. 'But you've never spoken to me like this before.' True, he hadn't. And hasn't since either. I played the piece till I got it right and learnt two important lessons that day. One on the piano and the other etched forever in my mind – that I shouldn't confuse Papi's affections for a lack of authority. If he's being liberal with me, I should be responsible with, and respect that liberty.

'You must give respect to earn respect' – it's not just a hollow saying. But very often parents erroneously expect respect

because he is… ❧ *98*

Papi's love for music and the arts enriched my childhood too. Papi encouraged me to take lessons in sitar, Kathak, piano and ballet. The piano stayed with me the longest.

This was one of our Sundays, with Papi's friends, my friends and a monkey dance for amusement.

from their children just because they're parents. What the child really feels is probably more fear than respect. Papi respected me as an individual even while I was a toddler and, as a result, I have grown up with a tremendous sense of respect for the person he is – not only because he is my father. One time, my ayah and driver took me to the Centaur Hotel for swimming instead of Sea Rock Hotel where I usually went. We had membership in both places. Papi looked for me at Sea Rock and didn't find me there. When we returned, he asked the driver where we'd gone. The driver told him I'd insisted on going to Centaur, which I denied because I hadn't. Papi asked me, '*Aap jhoot bolte hain*?' (Are you lying?) With a very sullen face I said, '*Hum jhoot nahin bolte.*' (I don't lie.)

Papi narrated this incident to me during the

Papi has nurtured me gently through the years … keeping me close at all times…

course of our chats for this book. Then he asked me if I ever remembered him using that phrase '*Aap jhoot bolte hain?*' with me in all these years. He said he'd decided on that day itself to never ask me this question again – because in my eyes he had seen that I was hurt by his suspicion and disbelief. And he didn't. I don't remember him ever asking me this question in my entire conscious memory.

But I can't say that I have never lied to Papi. Like most children, I too have spoken my share of white lies during the 'turbulent teen' years. As I got older, somewhere inside me I began to realize that you really can't fool your parents. They know you, and they know…

For example, Papi once said to me very casually, 'You know that holiday you went on with Meeta, to Delhi? I knew then that you were actually going to meet your boyfriend, Govind.'

Govind, who is now my husband, and I exchanged very sheepish glances. And somehow, I didn't want to deny it.

And Papi said, 'I knew, but I trusted you, and I wanted you to know that I trusted you. That's why I never questioned you.'

Papi would often take me to Juhu beach on Sundays, to romp in the sea.

And he didn't. For nine years.

Swimming was one of my favourite outings. Papi would take me to the Sea Rock Hotel where we were members of the Playmate Club. Sometimes after school or on weekends, Papi would take me to the local bookstore with him where we would both buy books. Some Sundays we'd even go to Juhu beach and romp in the sea, which used to be much cleaner then.

Sundays have always been a special day with Papi as he would really shut off from all his work and spend it with me. Even now, when I'm older and married, Papi, Govind and I have brunch together, if nothing more, most Sundays.

Sunday is also the day Papi likes to pamper himself, not that he has an opulent lifestyle otherwise. He spends more time at the Bandra Gymkhana, playing additional games of tennis and sometimes having breakfast with his friends there. He gets a massage from the maalishwala who comes home. His other loyal old-timer is his nai Atiullah who comes twice a week to shave Papi's trademark stubble. Papi doesn't shave himself and hasn't done so in thirty years. This and the fact that his kurtas are not washed at home but are laundered because of the crisp starching that he likes are perhaps Papi's only extravagances. Sometimes the kurtas are so heavily starched that they tear while he tries to wear them!

Papi prefers to shave like this – in his balcony by his nai (barber) of over thirty years, Atiullah. In the picture is Atiullah's son who takes over when Atiullah goes to his hometown on his annual leave.

Dr Hussain Taylor, another one of Papi's close friends whom he met at the Bandra Gymkhana. They both 'defected' together, from badminton to tennis!

Ashok of Ashok Tailors in Santa Cruz has been making Papi's kurtas for decades, keeping it unchanged in spite of fashion trends. On Sundays, Papi generally wears a *salwar-kurta* instead of his regular kurta and pants, which are also given a break from the week.

Papi really unwinds on Sundays. He rarely naps in the afternoons on other days of the week. And he is very possessive about the time that he needs for himself on this one day of the week. In fact, he and Rahi uncle have even had a tiff about it. Sundays would be Rahi uncle's day off too and that's when he would want to get out of his house and spend the day over at Papi's, while Papi, having worked and had meetings and spoken to people through the week, would want solitude and quiet on Sundays. So one fateful Sunday, Rahi uncle was refused a visit; Papi told him he didn't want to see anybody. 'Not even me?' asked Rahi uncle. 'Not even you,' replied Papi. Childlike as he was, Rahi uncle took it to heart and started sending Papi notes and telegrams that read: 'Save friends. Spare Sundays' and 'Friendship is for six days a week.' Naturally, Papi didn't let him brood for too long and they had quite a few Sundays together after that.

Papi with his gang at the Bandra Gymkhana. It may seem unusual but quite a few of Papi's closest friends are not even remotely connected with films.

Till Rahi uncle succumbed to illness and passed away in April 2001.

In December 2001, Papi lost another dear friend, Dr Hussain Taylor who, I remember, spoke in between his laughs instead of the other way round! Papi met Dr Taylor at the Bandra Gymkhana in the 1980s when he had just started going there. Before that, Papi used to play badminton in the compound of Jeetendra's bungalow till a building was constructed there; and also in the compound of the bungalow next to Papi's bungalow, 'Boskyana'. Before he joined the Bandra Gymkhana, Papi also played in the court of a hostel near Mehboob Studios in Bandra, till it closed for renovation. In his search for another court, he came upon the Bandra Gymkhana where he met Mr Thampi Koshy, who helped him get membership there. Papi soon became a part of the gymkhana's badminton gang. Dr Taylor played badminton there too and got along famously with Papi because of his humorous nature as well as his deep love for Urdu.

In between the games of badminton, Papi would go to the tennis courts outside and watch the ongoing games. Having played cricket in school, Papi had an instinct for catching the ball and

Dr Taylor with his wife, whom I call 'Aapaa', and daughter, at my wedding.

would often end up behaving like a ballboy on the tennis courts. Soon he bought himself a racket and started playing tennis intermittently. His friends from the badminton gang tried to dissuade him, saying they were two different games, one played from the wrist, the other from the elbow; playing both would affect both his game as well as his arm. It was only Dr Kothari, also a friend from the Bandra Gymkhana, who rubbished the warnings, saying that it was all in the mind. So Papi continued with tennis. Dr Taylor felt envious and joined Papi in tennis too. Soon tennis became the preferred game and badminton, the in-between game, which it still is.

Papi and Dr Taylor became very close friends, driving together to the gymkhana every morning for close to seventeen years. Dr Taylor and his wife, whom Govind and I call 'Aapaa', were an integral part of my wedding ceremony too and blessed us with the *Imaam Zamin,* a holy amulet tied around the arm for divine protection. The line between being friends or family blurred with the years.

Papi is not a very religious man. He indulges in religious customs and rituals more as a culturally enriching experience, rather than for their religious significance. The only ritual he has unfailingly observed over the years is the havan that is performed every year on my birthday. Our family pujaari, Anshuman*ji*, conducts the havan, which generally takes place early in the morning and ends with Papi blessing me and giving me my

Papi used to have Holi get-togethers at his house, with his friends and mine – till the tedium of washing off the colour took over from the revelry.

The havan performed each year on my birthday is perhaps the only religious ritual that Papi observes ... religiously! Seen here on my seventh and twenty-fourth birthdays.

birthday gift for that year. Even Papi's choice of birthday gifts has grown along with me – he gave me my first video camera at seventeen (subsequently updated with newer models every few years), my first ATM card to my own bank account when I was eighteen, my first still camera at twenty-two and, most recently, my laptop. But most precious are the children's books he wrote for me; he would present the first copy to me at the end of the havan, every year, till I was thirteen.

Another regular celebration was Holi – not because he enjoyed it, but because I loved it. He would call his friends and their families over, my friends would be there too and we would all be in the lawn of the house, smothering each other with gulaal and feasting on samosas and jalebis. His Holi get-togethers stopped as I grew out of the festival. I now find it too abrasive, getting doused with colours and unknown substances and then the tedium of washing it off.

Diwali, however, is still a favourite. We'd light fourteen diyas around the house together, both in Ma's

Papi enjoys lighting diyas and candles on Diwali – as long as the candles are not from his cherished collection!

and Papi's house. Ma would buy lots of crackers and fireworks which we'd set off on the road outside her house. Dinner would be at Ma's house sometimes and at Papi's at others. Now that I'm married, they both come over for dinner to my place, and we light candles instead of fireworks.

Interestingly, Papi has also observed the roza (the fast during the period of Ramzan) for a long period of his life. I have memories of sitting with him at the table during Iftaar as he ended his fast, sometimes accompanied by Bhooshan uncle and others. It is only now, during the course of writing this book that I learnt that Papi had promised Meena*ji* (Kumari) that he'd keep her rozas for her. Meena Kumari would religiously observe all her rozas each year, till her failing health required her to take medication regularly, thereby not allowing her to fast. Papi offered to observe the fasts for her, and did so each year, keeping all thirty of them, till his own blood-pressure problems put him on regular medication too.

There is so much of Papi that I have grown up with, so much I have lived with. And yet, I am only just beginning to learn ... and understand.

Papi used to keep all thirty rozas (fasts) during Ramzan, and break the fast with khajoor (dates) as is the custom, during iftaar.

Papi and I, lighting diyas at his house on Diwali.

na – na, rehne do, mat mitao inhe
in lakeeron ko yun hi rehne do
nanhe-nanhe gulaabi haathon se
mere maasoom nanhe bachche ne
tedhi-medhi lakeeren kheenchi hain
kya hua 'shakl' ban saki na agar
mere bachche ke haath hain in mein
meri pehchaan hai lakeeron mein

'*Drawing*' – PUKHRAAJ

moondrops on celluloid…

Around 1976, Papi started his own film production company under the banner of Meghna Movies so that he could continue to make his kind of films without any interference or pressure from outside producers. Papi had already experienced the fickleness of film producers by then. He had launched *Devdas* with popular actors Dharmendra, Hema Malini and Sharmila Tagore. It was being produced by Kailash Chopra, brother of famous movie 'villain' Prem Chopra. Papi felt that in both the previous versions of the film, having legendary actors like K.L. Saigal and Dilip Kumar in the title role had somewhat overshadowed the female characters. An ardent admirer of Sharat Chandra's work, Papi felt that the fine nuances in the original characters of the female protagonists, Paro and Chandramukhi, had remained undressed in the film versions. Paro was a girl who turned into a woman overnight, while Chandramukhi, the courtesan, was a woman on the farther side of youth who fell hopelessly in love with Devdas, as a young girl would. Devdas himself was the only one who could not get out of the orbit of adolescence. Hence, the choice of Dharmendra for the role. Papi feels that Dharmendra has always been an adolescent at heart, and still is!

Papi had shot scenes in Chandramukhi's kotha (courtesan's chamber) with Sharmila Tagore as well as some scenes of Paro at Devdas's house, between Hema Malini and Dharmendra. Two songs had also been recorded for the film with Papi's favourite – R.D. Burman. Then, for reasons best known to him, the producer backed out of the project.

This probably led Papi to believe that being his own producer would avoid such misfortune. Film producer Pranlal Mehta got into a partnership with Papi to oversee the production side of Meghna Movies so that Papi could concentrate on his creativity. To establish the banner, a commercially viable proposition was

Papi had launched *his* version of *Devdas* with Hema Malini as Paro and Dharmendra in the title role, but unfortunately, the film never got completed.

needed – and Papi launched *Kinaara* with Jeetendra and Hema Malini first and then *Kitaab* later.

Kinaara was shot extensively at Mandu, an ancient fortified city, a few hours' drive from Indore, Madhya Pradesh, once again reiterating Papi's penchant for ruins and ancient monuments. 'Monuments in ruins have a history and a sense of nostalgia about them ... the fascinating stories that can be found among the ruins instigate the imagination ... on every visit!' Papi says. The ruins of Mandu are famous for its legends of Princess Roopmati and Bazbahadur. Papi has frequented Mandu many times; it was a routine stopover during his many road trips from Bombay to Delhi. And we celebrated his sixty-seventh birthday there too.

But back in the mid-1970s, Papi's aversion to maths and number-crunching was once again validated as his production company, Meghna Movies, came under serious financial trouble, leaving Papi with no rights or negatives to either

It would be interesting to see Papi's interpretation of the classic *Devdas,* particularly in the present time ... Sharmila Tagore as Chandramukhi.

Kinaara was the first film under Papi's own production banner, 'Meghna Movies'. Once again, Jeetendra was not allowed to go without a moustache!

film, but a huge debt as well. Since then, Papi has sworn off film production and as he says, 'spared my creativity!'

In spite of the financial debacle, *Kitaab* remains one of Papi's favourite films, also because it gave him an opportunity to work with Uttam Kumar, Bengal's legendary matinee idol. Papi says Uttam Kumar was effortless – as a person and as an actor. When Papi called to offer him the film, he agreed on the phone itself. *Kitaab* also had the child actor, Master Raju, who had begun his film career with Papi's *Parichay* when he was barely three, and almost grew up in Papi's films. With *Kitaab,* Papi says he gained more confidence over the medium of films – he began to handle the camera himself, even though he used to operate the camera in his earlier films too, for songs and musical sequences. However, he feels his earlier films were very talkative, he was more of a writer but with *Kitaab,* he gradually began to gain more confidence as a director.

The writer, however, was not too far behind – Papi's third book of poems, *Kuchh aur Nazmein,* was published in 1980 by

Radhakrishna Prakashan. His second book, *Ek Boond Chaand,* came out in the mid-1970s but it had only a few poems more than his previous *book, Jaanam. Kuchh aur Nazrnein* was fuller, with many new poems, as well as some from the previous two books.

During Papi's final days at Bimal Roy Productions, along with working on the script for *Amrit Kumbh ki Khoj,* Papi also wrote the script of *Do Dooni Chaar.* Bimal*da*'s health was failing but Papi and his colleagues did not want Bimal Roy Productions to close down during Bimal*da*'s lifetime at least. So they all took voluntary cuts in their salaries and launched *Do Dooni Chaar,* to be directed by Debu Sen. United Producers, a conglomerate of film producers who were friends of Bimal*da,* helped to oversee the making of the film. However, Papi feels that somehow the film was not as completely realized as it had been conceived, that it fell short in spite of having a good script. This feeling stayed with Papi – he was sure he could make a better film of it and offered to remake it, to a couple of producers. Till Mr Jai Singh came around – he was a businessman venturing into production and Shakespeare's *A Comedy of Errors* had been his favourite play since his college days. He immediately took up Papi's offer and *Angoor* was made in 1980. Even Sanjeev Kumar was relieved that he wasn't playing an old man and Papi was finally making a light-hearted film!

Kuchh aur Nazmein … Papi's fourth book was published in 1980.

Sanjeev Kumar was the only actor whose unpunctuality on the sets Papi would overlook, because Papi always kept his physical condition in consideration. During the making of *Namkeen* in 1981, the band of ladies comprising the gifted actors Waheeda Rehman, Sharmila Tagore, Shabana Azmi and Kiran Vairale often protested this partiality. They teased Papi that he would put up banners on the back of the reflectors – *Punctuality is a moral responsibility* – if any of them was even slightly late, but would

Angoor was Papi's only light-hearted comedy ... and for once, Sanjeev Kumar was not playing an old man, much to his relief as well. Moushumi Chatterjee ably matched Sanjeev Kumar's comic timing too.

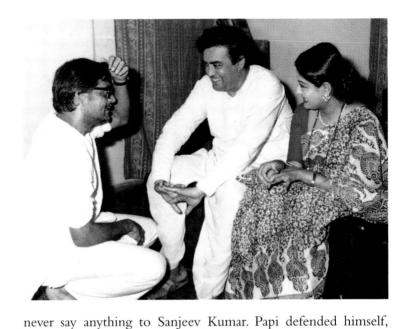

Papi's partiality towards Sanjeev Kumar's lack of punctuality had become a bone of contention on the sets of *Namkeen*. But Sanjeev Kumar would give one effortless shot, and the four women would be in his corner!

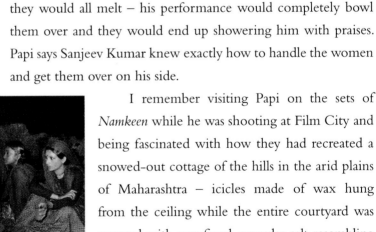

never say anything to Sanjeev Kumar. Papi defended himself, suggesting that since they were in a majority they should unite and take up the matter with Sanjeev Kumar themselves. Which they did: every time Sanjeev Kumar came late, all of them sulked and did not really talk to him. Till he would give his first shot and they would all melt – his performance would completely bowl them over and they would end up showering him with praises. Papi says Sanjeev Kumar knew exactly how to handle the women and get them over on his side.

I remember visiting Papi on the sets of *Namkeen* while he was shooting at Film City and being fascinated with how they had recreated a snowed-out cottage of the hills in the arid plains of Maharashtra – icicles made of wax hung from the ceiling while the entire courtyard was covered with unrefined, granular salt resembling fallen snow. Years later, I saw the film again, as an adult *and* a film-maker and was once again

Namkeen was an intriguing play of varied relationships at different planes, all running simultaneously.

fascinated, this time by the relationships in the film. There was no one-on-one relationship in the entire film except in the end, between Sanjeev Kumar and Sharmila Tagore. The film was woven with triangles and squares of relationships — each scene always had more than two characters in it — and if one left, leaving just two characters in the scene, another appeared to complete the triangle or square.

Papi's inclination to explore facets of various relationships through his films led him to delve into yet another mystical bond — that of Meera and Lord Krishna. Prem*ji* had been a production controller for Bimal Roy Productions before he became an independent producer himself. He had also been a part of IPTA and PWA and, Papi says, was very up to date with his reading and general knowledge. He offered Papi to make a film based on Meera, with two preconditions — actor Hema Malini and music directors Laxmikant–Pyarelal. Papi was most fascinated by the aspect of a princess's journey from her palace to the ektara — how she became a poetess and a lover of Krishna. He had done a lot

Papi had done extensive research on Meera before he wrote the film, which was produced by Premji (second from right). The research was then published for future reference.

of research on Meera as he wanted to make a historical film, not a mythology, and even had his research published for future reference. Papi's major source of information was a book titled *Annals and Antiquities of Rajasthan* by Col. James Todd.

Around 1980–81, when *Meera* was being planned, legendary singer Lata Mangeshkar had just released an album of Meera's bhajans composed by her brother, Hridaynath Mangeshkar. She felt it would be repetitive to do the playback for a film on Meera as well. Since Lata Mangeshkar had refused to sing for the film, no music director, including Laxmikant–Pyarelal, was willing to be part of the project, fearing the legendary singer's disapproval. Papi knew he had to find someone who was above the politics of the film industry.

His search ended in New York where sitar maestro Pandit Ravi Shankar was touring at the time.

Papi had never worked with Pandit Ravi Shankar before but had admired his work in the film *Anuradha* and his compositions of our two national songs. Pandit Ravi Shankar's only condition was

Papi's film on the legendary poetess Meera was 'not a mythology', as he says, 'but historical. It traces the journey of a princess from her palace to the ektara.'

that he should like the script and that he would meet Papi when he returned to India in September, which was a few months away. When Papi insisted on flying over to New York right away to meet him, Pandit Ravi Shankar remarked, 'You seem very confident of your script!' Papi met Pandit Ravi Shankar in New York and, over two sittings, he approved Papi's script and asked for the songs he had to compose. Papi wanted to be involved in the composition of the songs, as he is for all his films. Pandit Ravi Shankar said he was touring and Papi offered to travel along! So my father accompanied him on a few of his concerts and they worked on the songs for *Meera* as well. Papi returned to India and then waited for Pandit Ravi Shankar to arrive in India in September.

When Pandit Ravi Shankar arrived that September, he recorded the entire soundtrack of *Meera* – about seven songs and some pieces of background music as well – in about two weeks!

R.D, Burman had also refrained from getting embroiled in any controversy, especially because of his relations with the Mangeshkar family (he was married to Asha Bhosle, who was also

In his footsteps ... Papi and I in Bangalore – I accompanied him on one of his writing trips.

Lata Mangeshkar's sister), and declined to compose the music for *Meera*. His association with Papi, however, continued in his other films as well as in films like *Doosri Sita*, *Baseraa* and others made by other directors for which Papi wrote the songs.

Papi has also had the privilege of writing the script for the debut film of many notable directors – *Andaaz* for Ramesh Sippy, *New Delhi Times* for Ramesh Sharma, *Gharonda* for Bhimsain, *Hip Hip Hurray* for Prakash Jha, *Ek Pal* for Kalpana Lajmi and *Masoom* for Shekhar Kapoor, among many others.

Papi often went to Bangalore to write scripts and always stayed at the Westend Hotel, in room no. 50 ... each time! I accompanied him when he went to write *Masoom*. We had a wonderful time there together – swimming, playing and shopping. It was in Bangalore, probably on an earlier trip, that I met and became friends with Gargi, daughter of film directors Vikas Desai and Aruna Raje. Gargi was almost my age – but she didn't live to be as old as I am today.

Gargi succumbed to cancer when she was ten. Her parents had not hidden her condition from her and she knew she did not

Gargi and I in Bangalore.

Papi's writing is ceaseless ... in scripts, short stories and poems.

have very long to live. Her favourite comic book was *Superman*. Papi once heard her remark: 'Even God is like Superman ... he can do anything ... but only in books...'

Papi was very stung with this observation from one so young. He wrote a story on Gargi, titled 'Gargi and Superman', picking up a moment of life that had touched him and preserving it through his creativity. The book Papi wrote for my tenth birthday was dedicated to Gargi.

His ink flows tirelessly – in film scripts, screenplays, lyrics, short stories and poems. But Papi values the recognition he gets in the field of literature more than any laurels he may achieve for his work in films. He glows with pride every time a new book of his is published, even though there have been many by now. For him, each time is like the first time.

He especially cherishes the publication of *Dastakhat*, his collection of Urdu short stories that was first published in Pakistan around 1989 by noted Urdu poet Janaab Ahmed Nadeem Qasmi, whom Papi fondly calls Baba. The association grew into a very

Janaab Ahmed Nadeem Qasmi (Baba) with his daughter Mansoora.

close yet peculiar relationship – they spoke over the phone at least a couple of times a week, sharing everyday happenings and special occasions alike. His daughter Mansoora is also very close to Papa – I call her Khaalaa (aunt). Yet none of us ever met in fourteen years! Till Qasmi saab fell ill in 2004, and Papi had to rush to Pakistan to visit him. It is best to hear about this meeting in Papi's own words as he described it to a journalist in *Outlook*:

Baba was admitted to the hospital and I was informed that he was suffering from a heart disease. I immediately decided to apply for a Pakistani visa. I called the Pakistan consulate. The guy asked me when I wanted to visit Pakistan. Tomorrow morning, I replied. It was Sunday the next day and the Pakistan consulate was closed. But he said: 'I am well aware of your desire to meet Ahmed Nadeem Qasmi. I understand your feelings and respect your emotions. I will open the consulate office tomorrow at 11 a.m. only for one hour to arrange for your visa. Meanwhile, you should rush to Delhi as soon as possible.'

How I reached Delhi is a story in itself. I was granted a four-day emergency visa the very next day at 11 a.m. I was told not to appear before the media and was barred from giving interviews to newspapers and television. I promised to stay away from the media.

Shahzad Rafique, a friend, was waiting for me at Lahore airport. He took me straight to the hospital where Qasmi sahab was admitted. It was the year 2004. Emotionally stressed, I stepped inside the room. I saw him lying on the bed. They were doing his medical check-up. Since Qasmi sahab was a big name in Pakistan, ministers frequently visited him in the hospital. The only issue was that the media followed them. I knew that I had to stay away from the media. Various newspapers and channels tried to contact me for interviews but Shahzad Rafique handled the situation very tactfully. Despite all our efforts, my pictures were published in the newspapers and I was seen in the news on the television too.

After two days, Baba was discharged from the hospital and we took him back home. This was my first meeting with Baba. I returned to India after four days, only to learn that Baba had fallen ill again. One day I got the news that he had left us.

Baba ke saath meri pehli mulaaqaat hi akhri thi. Doosri mulaqaat main ab kar ke aya hoon jo zaroori reh gayi thi. Uske baghair daayra toota sa mehsoos hota tha (My first meeting with him was my last. The second meeting I just had, which was essential. Without it, the circle seemed broken somehow).

Baba also published Papi's collection of poems, *Chand Pukhraaj Ka*, which was later published in 1994, in Hindi as *Pukhraaj* and in English as *Silences. Dastakhat* was published in India in 1997 as *Dhuaan* in Urdu and *Raavi Paar* in Hindi, English, Bengali, Marathi and even Punjabi.

When Papi introduced a new form of poetry in Urdu, called 'Triveni', Baba was Papi's most vocal supporter and source of encouragement as he had been with all of his writing. The form of the 'Triveni' is such that the first two lines are a complete couplet in itself. The third line – which forms the 'Triveni' – complements the couplet and also gives it a whole new twist. These were first published around 1972–73 in a magazine called *Sarika* which was edited by Kamleshwar. It was published as a collection called *Triveni* in 2001.

Along with his poems and short stories, Papi is also very proud of the books that he regularly writes for children – the thirteen he wrote for me which includes *Bosky ki Ginti, Bosky*

Papi loves to write for children – in fact, he loves anything to do with children. He wrote *Kaayda*, the Hindi alphabet in verse, for Aarushi, a children's organization in Bhopal.

ke Gappein, Bosky ke Aasman and *Bosky ka Panchatantra,* which are tales of the Panchatantra written in verse for children to sing. He has also written *Kaayda,* the Hindi alphabet in verse, for Aarushi, a children's foundation in Bhopal. The illustrations in this book have been done by the children themselves. He has written various scholastic books like *Ek Mein Do, Paaji Baadal, Suno Kahaani* and *Ek Ghar, Naam Saal* which describes the twelve months of the year in verse, using the analogy of twelve guests living in one house.

Interestingly, Papi's writing has never taken a back seat to his film work. In fact, he would sometimes deliberately space out film projects to make time for his writing – his first love, as he calls it.

After a gap of a few years after *Meera,* Papi made *Ijaazat* around 1986, with the graceful Rekha and the gifted Naseeruddin Shah. It remains one of my favourite films till today – purely for the grace and humaneness with which Papi dealt with infidelity and extramarital relationship.

On location for *Ijaazat* with
Naseeruddin Shah and Rekha.

Naseeruddin Shah had been harbouring a dream for years ... to play Ghalib. When he got the opportunity to play the role in Papi's *Mirza Ghalib*, he virtually embodied the very being of Ghalib.

With Naseeruddin Shah, Papi formed a wonderful creative association that produced one of the finest works in both their careers – the TV serial, *Mirza Ghalib*. Papi always says, 'Ghalib had three faithful servants – Kallu, his maid Wafaadaar who stammered, and me!' Such a devoted servant was he that he actually waived his fees as writer and director to keep the budget of the serial under control. He was compensated with the rights to the serial, which the producers considered expendable. But Papi's loyalty paid off – in royalties from the satellite and music rights of the serial! Even the most discerning of ghazal connoisseurs concur that the soundtrack of *Mirza Ghalib* is perhaps the finest of all time. Papi feels that it is also one of Jagjit Singh's finest works as a singer and composer. Even though the renowned Jagjit Singh and many other singers had sung Ghalib before, singing to a situation to make a desired impact greatly affects the composition as well as the rendering.

Interestingly, Papi had announced a film on Ghalib with Sanjeev Kumar as the poet, over a decade before he actually made the TV serial. Unfortunately, the film was never realized.

Ghazal singers Jagjit Singh and Chitra with Papi at the launch of the soundtrack of *Mirza Ghalib*. To date, the album is considered one of Jagjit Singh's finest works.

It took years, but Papi never abandoned the dream ... and fulfilled his desire to document the life of the legendary poet Mirza Ghalib, with his TV serial *Mirza Ghalib*.

But Naseeruddin Shah's dream of playing Ghalib was eventually and ironically fulfilled.

When Papi had announced the film, Naseer, as Papi calls him, was still in college. He had written to Papi asking him not to make Ghalib with Sanjeev Kumar, as he was slightly overweight and didn't fit the character. When the film was not made, Naseeruddin Shah assumed that Papi had taken his advice. When Sanjeev Kumar lost weight a few years later, Naseer was in the National School of Drama. Fearing that maybe now the film would be resurrected, he once again wrote to Papi asking him to wait till he reached the Bombay film industry as an actor. Such was his frantic desire to play Ghalib! And when Papi finally offered the part to him for the serial, he reminded Papi of the letters he'd written to him years ago saying, 'I'm now convinced that you can't make Ghalib without me and no one can play him better than me!'

Amazingly, Naseeruddin Shah had never brought up this incident earlier, when they worked together on *Ijaazat* or even *Libaas*.

On the sets of *Libaas* –
Papi's '*asamaapt kavita*'!

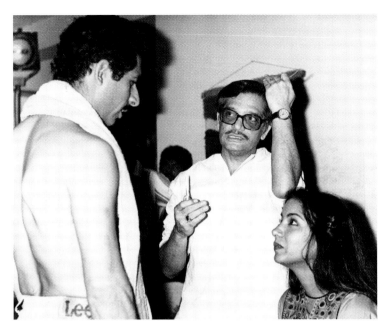

Libaas is another of Papi's favourite films and his last film
soundtrack with Pancham uncle. He says the most interesting facet
about *Libaas* is that it is about relationships between actors – they
are not men and women, but just actors. And these actors react
and perform a certain way in fictional situations, on stage. But
when similar incidents happen in their real lives, their reactions
and responses are completely different. He still rues the fact that
it has not been released – once again underscoring the fact that
a producer with conviction is crucial to a film – like Sippy saab
used to be.

Libaas was finally screened
at the IFFI, Goa, recently.
Seen here with Vishal and
Rekha at the screening.

When Lata Mangeshkar decided to turn
producer, it stemmed purely from the desire to
make a film that had good music and good songs.
Papi says she was fed up of singing substandard
songs. In their conversations, the element of
the supernatural and the unexplained would
keep coming up. In those days, the new Dalai

Lama was also born in Spain, just as the former Dalai Lama had predicted before dying. Several inexplicable cases of supposed reincarnation were being printed in magazines like the *Illustrated Weekly*, etc. All of this was happening in the twentieth century, and the educated and the intellectuals were accepting it, albeit with some degree of scepticism – conversations and statements often ending with '*Lekin…*' (But...)

Papi was once again working with one of his dear friends, Vinod Khanna, who had just returned to films after his time with Osho. The gorgeous Dimple Kapadia perfectly embodied the haunting 'Rewa', the tormented spirit in the film. Her searching eyes continue to gaze at you long after the film is over. I don't know if many people realized – Papi had not let Dimple blink throughout the film. He says it would make her real. Not blinking, with an endless, fixed gaze gave her a feeling of being surreal.

The shooting of *Lekin* was also marked with injuries – most unusual and both off the sets of the film. During one schedule, Papi fractured his ankle getting out of bed, which is just a mattress on the floor, about five inches high. And on another schedule, Papi was called away from the shoot as I had met with

At the mahurat of *Lekin* – a film that evolved from a desire for quality music in films. It was produced by the legendary Lata Mangeshkar, and its soundtrack has one of her finest singing.

With Manmohan
Singh (Man*ji*) – Papi's
cinematographer
and friend.

an accident trying to ride a motorcycle with my friend Meeta.
Both times, Papi was shooting at Mehboob Studios in Bandra.

This was also Papi's first film with Manmohan Singh as
cinematographer, though they had already done *Mirza Ghalib*
together by now. Papi especially praises 'Man*ji*'s' (as we all call
Manmohan Singh) sense of music and timing in operating the
camera. Being quite a good singer himself, there is an inherent
rhythm and grace in Man*ji*'s cinematography. He's always calm in
temperament and often hums to himself – a very big asset to any
director. Any jitters I had during the shooting of my first film,
Filhaal..., would melt away as soon as Man*ji* came on to the sets.

Lekin fulfilled the purpose for which it was made – its music
score by Hridaynath Mangeshkar was exquisite and became very
successful. It won all the three National awards for music in 1991
– music director, singer and lyrics!

The Filmfare Awards of 1990 were also very memorable –
Ma won the trophy for Best Supporting Actress for *Ram Lakhan,*
It was a touching moment for me to see Papi announce the award
and call out to the winner saying, '*Aji sunti ho!*'

They still laugh together ...
January 2000

haath chhooten bhi toh rishte nahin chhoda karte
waqt ki shaakh se lamhe nahin toda karte...

Maraasim

woh jo shaayar tha...

Papi directing Om Puri, on the sets of his TV serial based on literary short stories, *Kirdaar.*
Om Puri played the main protagonist in each story.

Literature has always been a treasure chest of inspiration for Papi's creativity. After *Lekin…* in 1993, Papi made yet another TV serial, *Kirdaar*, based on literary short stories. The talented Om Puri played the protagonist in every story. Before that, Papi had also made two documentaries — one on sarod maestro Ustad Amjad Ali Khan in 1990 and the other on esteemed vocalist Pandit Bhimsen Joshi in 1992.

Papi was in Delhi to record some sarod pieces for the documentary on Ustad Amjad Ali Khan and didn't know the way to the recording studio. He called the studio and someone gave him directions. The person then asked where Papi was and offered to pick him up and bring him to the studio. That was Papi's first meeting with composer and film-maker Vishal Bhardwaj. Vishal had been waiting at the studio all day just to meet Papi!

When Vishal moved to Bombay to pursue a career as a music director for films, he once again called on Papi. They worked together on a few jingles and title songs for TV serials and made their first mark as a team with '*Chaddi pehen ke phool khila hai*', the title song of the TV serial *The Jungle Book*. Such is the dynamism of Papi and Vishal's collaboration that when Disney's feature film, *The Jungle Book*, was released in Hindi in 2016, the same song was re-recorded and included in the trailer of the film!

It was Vishal who introduced Papi to R.V. Pandit, who owned the music company CBS where Vishal earlier worked. Papi was contemplating making a film on some contemporary social situation. Papi has continuously tried to let the childhood scars from the Partition breathe through his writings, but he now felt more confident as a director and mature as a person to make a

During the shoots of Papi's two national award-winning documentaries profiling renowned vocalist Pandit Bhimsen Joshi and esteemed sarod player, Ustad Amjad Ali Khan.

film on a subject that was also very close to his emotional core. As if by providence, R.V. Pandit was also very socially conscious and had done a lot of writing on the subject of terrorism in Punjab, among other things. When Papi narrated the idea to Pandit*ji*, he enthusiastically agreed to produce the film. And *Maachis* was lit…

Naturally, Vishal was to score the music. It was the first time Papi was working with another music director for his film after Pancham uncle's death and I often wonder if Vishal found the pressure daunting. Papi says there were initial teething problems as very few music directors are sensitive to the film as a whole, along with the music they compose, like R.D. Burman was.

But these soon gave way to a very successful creative collaboration as the music of *Maachis* met with stupendous success. '*Chappa chappa charkha chale*' was played in paan shops and discotheques alike. Interestingly, the song was shot in just

Vishal Bhardwaj (second from right) was instrumental in introducing Papi to R.V. Pandit (fifth from right) who went on to produce *Maachis*.

four hours – the location site in Manali had been snowed out and three shooting days had been lost. They had just one day to shoot the song before the snow melted and the landscape changed completely. It was only Manmohan Singh's sheer ingenuity that he and Papi could re-choreograph the whole song and shoot it in four hours.

Beneath the Rockefeller Tree. Papi had taken a break from the shooting of *Maachis* to spend Christmas with me – New York, 1995.

That year, 1995, I celebrated my birthday in the skies as Papi and I flew back to New York – I was returning for my course in film production at New York University and he was taking a break from shooting to spend Christmas with me. Papi had carried the rough track of '*Chhod aaye hum woh galiyaan*'. It was so fresh and energetic, yet there was so much anger and pain seething below the surface of the song. Most of the songs of *Maachis* are drenched in a subdued anguish.

My first reaction to the choice of the male lead, Chandrachur Singh, was complete disapproval. He didn't *look* like a hero. It was only when I saw the first cut, through brimming eyes, that I realized he'd been the right choice from the start. As was each and every other actor – Jimmy Shergil, Ravi Gosain, Suniel Sinha, Om Puri and, of course, Tabu.

Papi and Tabu share a wonderful relationship – she calls him 'Daddy' and he pampers her like a daughter. He says she is a very involved and thinking actor who gets under the skin of the character and lives the part rather than just performing it. It was only natural that when I made my first film, Tabu was a part of it.

Papi directing Chandrachur Singh and Tabu on the sets of *Maachis*.

With Tabu – she calls him 'Daddy' and he dotes on her like a father…

Well-known theatre personality Salim Arif was Papi's associate director in *Maachis*. He had worked with Papi as the costume designer in the serial *Mirza Ghalib*. *Maachis* onwards he has been an integral part of Papi's team, along with renowned sound designer Narinder Singh.

I joined Papi in the post-production of *Maachis* after I returned from New York in the summer of 1996. By then I was sure I wanted to be a film-maker. I had already assisted noted film-maker Saeed Mirza on *Naseem* before leaving for New York. I didn't want to begin with Papi as I knew practically nothing about film-making and being the director's daughter would come in the way of a complete hands-on learning experience. When I had learnt the basics, I was ready to assist Papi, as Papi says, on a loan from Saeed saab!

It was around the same time that I announced another important decision – I had found the man I would marry, Govind Singh Sandhu. I had known Govind since college and we had been seeing each other for two years by then. I was hesitant to tell Papi myself, so Ma broke the news to him. I met him in his office later to tell him the *whole* story. As always, it was Papi's demeanour of being a father and a friend that made the otherwise difficult moment simple and easy. He may have been wary of my decision and my choice – every parent is likely to be – I was twenty-three at the time, but I would always be his little girl. However, Papi was patient enough to get to know Govind instead of thwarting or dismissing him.

I was hesitant to tell Papi that I had met the man I wanted to marry ... with Govind in Germany.

Ma had already met Govind and liked him. Papi too took to Govind immediately and almost became like a surrogate father to him. Govind also looks upon Ma and Papi as parents rather than in-laws. He goes on agricultural excursions to plant nurseries and to the farm with Ma and has a maalish on Sunday afternoons with Papi. I guess Govind is more of the son that my parents had perhaps been missing.

The year 1996 ended on a pretty good note – I found my calling and my soulmate and *Maachis* was received with both critical and commercial success. So, the father and the film-maker rested a little easy...

In 1997, a new member was added to the Gulzar household – a male brindle Boxer whom we named Pali, after Chandrachur Singh's character in *Maachis*. Once, as a nine-year-old, I had brought home two Pomeranian puppies and, with the sweetest face I could make, asked Papi if we could keep them. Papi had no

After the release of *Maachis*, R.V. Pandit insisted on having this picture taken outside a theatre where it was playing. He wanted to prove film-trade experts wrong, who'd said, 'Gulzar's films don't work at the box office!'

He was named 'Pali' after Chandrachur Singh's character in *Maachis* and was a star in his own right! He was featured on the front page of the *Bombay Times* with a lost-and-found story, just like in the movies!

On an impulse, I had brought home two Pomeranian puppies and Papi very patiently agreed to keep them. With time, he too grew attached to them, till they passed on...

choice but to agree! Ma had always had dogs in her house, but Papi was not much of a dog person – till I added Chhotu and Motu, our two Pomeranians, to his home. With time, Papi got quite attached to them, especially to Chhotu after Motu's death when he was about seven. Chhotu lived till he was about fifteen – Papi used to call him 'buzurg' (elderly) and treat him like one too. After Chhotu passed away, Papi didn't have a dog for a few years, till Govind and I decided to get him another one. We had read an ad in the papers for Boxer puppies and went to find ourselves a puppy. One of the puppies in the litter was a perfect champion specimen, but I couldn't turn away from the one with a lopsided ear and clumsy look on his face – that was to be Pali! We were helplessly enamoured by Pali's sister too – the only female puppy left in the litter, and quite a greedy one. We named her Pari and she lived with Ma. A year later, Ma brought home Gabbar, a tiny Pug, who became Pari's companion and toy at the same time.

Pali had a definite routine – in sync with Papi's. He had his biscuits while Papi had his morning and evening tea. He would get an extra roti from Papi when Papi was finishing his dinner. Pali came downstairs when Papi would come down to his office, where Pali had an assigned place: his basket in the corner of the room. And while most other dogs would obey commands in English, Pali understood mostly Hindi because Papi spoke to him in Hindi. Papi would say, 'When you keep a dog, you automatically learn to speak English!'

One time, we almost lost Pali – someone had stolen him from right outside our gate. In those three traumatic days, many phone calls and enquiries were made, leaflets with Pali's picture on them were stuck around Bandra, and Pali even made it to the cover of *Bombay Times*! On reading that article, the person who had unknowingly bought Pali from the rogue, realized he

Pali's routine was almost synchronized with Papi's – he got his biscuits when Papi had tea, came down to the office with Papi and even went up only when Papi finished his workday!

was our missing dog and returned him to us. It is very rare that a lost or stolen pet finds its way back into your life, but it was almost as if Pali was destined to be a part of our family, and quite a star too. No camera crew that came to our house to shoot Papi could leave without taking a few shots of Pali too – he made his presence more than felt! Pali lived a full life with us, before he passed away nine years ago. Now, a ceramic figure of a sleeping boxer lies on a small mattress in the corner of Papi's office; just like Pali used to…

When Papi began work on *Hu Tu Tu* in 1998, I formally joined him as associate screenplay writer and intermittent assistant – as I was also doing independent work, making documentaries and music videos, and anchoring television shows. Papi's team of regulars was with him – Manmohan Singh, Narinder Singh, Salim Arif and Tabu. Due to personal reasons, Man*ji* could not attend some schedules of the shoot and cinematographer Rajen Kothari stepped in as the additional cinematographer. Since then, Rajen*ji* became a close friend and associate, bringing us mangoes from his

Left: The team in the early days – they all went on to become directors, but here, were Papi's assistants – (from left to right) N. Chandra, Meraj, Raj N. Sippy, R.L. Mishra and Sanjeev.

Right: Papi's film team later – (from left) cinematographer Manmohan Singh, close friend and associate Kailash Advani and sound designer Narinder Singh. Missing from the picture is Salim Arif, Papi's associate director.

farm every summer. In an uncanny replay, Rajen*ji* stepped in for Man*ji* for a few days during the shooting of *Filhaal...* Rajen*ji*'s passing away in 2012 was a deep loss for both Papi and me. But come summer, and the mangoes still arrive from his farm, brought by his son Pratik.

In *Hu Tu Tu*, Papi worked with Suniel Shetty and Nana Patekar for the first time. Suhasini Mulay returned to acting after decades and embodied the character of Malti Bai wonderfully. All of us braced the searing temperatures of rural Maharashtra where the film was largely shot. Nana Patekar even had a nose-bleed from the extreme heat. Govind too endured the heat when he visited us on location in Mahad. In *Hu Tu Tu*, I also experienced a plane ride, the thought of which still churns my stomach. We had to shoot a flight sequence as Suniel Shetty's character is a hobby flier. The influence and good graces of Mr Farokh Sarkari of Bhopal enabled us to shoot at Bhopal airport. Papi has known Farokh-bhai since the shooting of *Maachis* and he has come to be a close family friend as well as a cameo artist in Papi's films.

The sequence required shots of a Cessna aircraft taking off and landing. Real-life pilot Capt. Sethi was flying the aircraft in

Left: On location in Bhopal. I officially joined Papi as an assistant on *Hu Tu Tu.*

Right: Rajen Kothari was the additional cinematographer on *Hu Tu Tu* and has remained a colleague since.

Suniel Shetty's clothes while I was doubling for Tabu. The camera rolled, we took off, circled the airport and geared up for landing. The camera was placed almost in the middle of the runway, but the aircraft was to land safely, much before it. As the wheels of the aircraft touched the tarmac, Papi asked on the walkie-talkie, 'Can you take off again?' Capt. Sethi whispered under his breath, '*Pehle bolte toh achha hota*!' (It would have been nice if I was told a little earlier!) And he revved the engines to take off again. Straight ahead, the camera and the crew standing around it seemed to be closing in on us really fast. As the aircraft took off again, flying over the standing crew, I could see Man*ji* literally ducking!

Papi and the primary cast of *Hu Tu Tu* – Nana Patekar, Suniel Shetty and laadli Tabu.

Hu Tu Tu was a complex and layered film with many tracks running parallel as it dealt with the trials of a simple family journeying from the village to the city, getting caught in the dirty world of politics and the inevitable disillusionment and disintegration. It was an education working on the screenplay of *Hu Tu Tu* with Papi. However, as a director he worked solo – the shot breakdowns and other details would all be in his mind, with not much written on paper, nor open to discussion. This left me quite clueless sometimes, as with Saeed Mirza I was used to a more democratic way of working – everything was discussed and then tabulated on paper. Not wanting to disturb Papi, I would often take my questions to Salim (Arif) bhai, who would patiently answer them all. In all the years with Papi, he had understood Papi's way of thinking and working.

By the time *Hu Tu Tu* was released, I had already finished writing most of my second script and Papi was very keen that I start my film soon. Papi was very impressed with the idea of surrogate motherhood as an episode between two best friends – though I think and continue to believe that Papi is severely biased towards me, making him a little too generous in his praise. But somewhere deep inside me, it was this belief and pride he has in my capabilities that gave me the confidence to even dream of making a film.

Papi with long-time associate and friend Salim Arif, who helped me understand Papi's style of working on the sets of *Hu Tu Tu*.

I spent the whole of 1999 trying to get a producer and actors for my film. And Papi went through the struggle with me, as did Ma. But there would be times when things would really get to Papi. He would feel helpless and frustrated at not being able to provide me with a platform to launch my career – he didn't own a production banner that would produce my film unconditionally. I would goad him to start work on his film at least, but he would always say, 'Let your film take-off first.'

Another thought looming on Papi's mind was my marriage. I was very sure I wanted to get married only after I'd made one film. But Papi felt that the entire process of getting my film started was too precarious, with no real timeline, and as I was nearly twenty-six, it was the right age for me to get married. Govind too had just completed his MBA and joined Tata Consultancy Services.

Bosky byaahne ka ab waqt kareeb aane lagaa hai

jism se chhoot raha hai kuchh kuchh

rooh mein doob raha hai kuchh kuchh

kuchh udaasi hai, sukoon bhi

subah ka waqt hai pau phatne ka,

ya jhatpata shaam ka hai maloom nahin

yun bhi lagta hai ki jo mod bhi ab aayegaa

woh kisi aur taraf mud ke chali jaayegi

ugte hue sooraj ki taraf

aur main seedha hi kuchh door akelaa jaakar

shaam ke doosre sooraj mein samaa jaaunga!

'Bosky-1': *Raat Pashmine Ki*

The only one who calls Papi by his erstwhile pen-name 'Gautam', Papi's dear friend and associate, Kailash uncle - who was probably Papi's strongest pillar of help and support during my wedding.

I don't remember the exact moment or how it happened. I'm not even sure who first suggested the date – my parents, Govind's mother Geeta Sandhu, Govind or me – but somehow it was decided that Govind and I would get married in January 2000. My parents discussed the details with Geeta mama. Govind's father, Amarjit Singh Sandhu, had passed away when he was much younger. It so happened that Govind's brother Bharat's wedding to his then-girlfriend, Navneet, was fixed for November 1999. It was decided that Bharat's wedding would take place in Patiala where Govind's family lived, while we would get married in Bombay. So now, along with how and when my film would be made, Papi also worried about putting together my wedding.

The one person who was a tremendous help and support to him during this time was Kailash Advani, his long-time friend and erstwhile associate director. Papi has been friends with Kailash uncle since the mid-1950s, when he lived in Four Bungalows, and he is the only person who still calls Papi Gautam, the pen-name Papi had assumed for a short while before he went back to Gulzar. Kailash uncle is also probably the only person who has every book of Papi's that has been published, in any language – whether

My wedding was the exact opposite of Papi and Ma's chaotic and grand affair – it was simple and intimate – and took place in the garden of Papi's bungalow...

Our impromptu engagement in Patiala – Govind's mother Geeta Sandhu, Govind, Ma, I and Papi.

written by Papi or compiled by someone else. Papi says Kailash uncle doesn't even lend the books to him – Papi had wanted the copy of *Chauras Raat* once and Kailash uncle photocopied the entire book and gave it to him, but didn't give him the original.

Kailash uncle had already married off his daughter Pinky earlier, so he used all his experience and expertise to help Papi organize my wedding. Govind and I were very clear we wanted a small and simple wedding – nothing extravagant. Fortunately, both our families agreed and approved. Papi still reminisces how Kailash was the one person who would just keep asking for responsibilities and jobs to be done – *maang maang ke kaam leta tha!*

Papi, Ma, Govind and I went to Patiala in November 1999 for Bharat's wedding. In one of the pre-wedding dinners, Govind and I had an impromptu engagement, since we hadn't been formally engaged. In fact, even our wedding date was casually selected as the first convenient Sunday of January 2000. The first Sunday of January fell on the 2nd. The day after New Year was not acceptable – so we settled for the next Sunday – the 9th of January 2000. No planetary charts or panchaangs were consulted. And the rest of my wedding followed in a similar unconventional,

Ma and Papi dancing at my sangeet ... the way they came together during my wedding, as they have throughout my life – not for a moment did I feel that my parents were separated...

cosmopolitan yet sometimes traditional manner. We held an Akhand Paath in the gurudwara as per Sikh tradition, my haldi rituals were in the Bengali tradition, the mehendi and sangeet in Punjabi style with singers like Hariharan and Roopkumar Rathod livening up the occasion. We had Arya Samaji pheraas and a reception dinner with dancing and games as there are in Catholic weddings. Papi handled most of the organizational details, while Ma was in charge of rituals and tradition. Once again, at such a crucial juncture in my life, I never once felt like a child of separated parents – they came together like they always have ... for me...

I had made my parents promise that they would not cry during the wedding – Ma was sobbing uncontrollably. Papi tried to keep his promise, but I did catch a few tears escaping him too.

Papi had promised he wouldn't cry ... but now and then, I'd catch him wipe a stubborn tear from his eye...

For Papi, my wedding was not so much a closure or a parting. I'd always be close to him, emotionally and geographically. I had joked on the eve of my wedding, 'Don't get emotional, it's only a break of a few days for you. After that, I'll be right back to, "Papi, can I take the car, I have to go somewhere!"'

But Papi says the change comes from the fact that even though I would still be a part of his family, from this time on, I would be making a family of my own. 'When it's morning and I'm wondering if you have woken up in time for college or work, and I want to send a cup of tea to your room, you won't be in that room anymore ... that's the thought that hurts,' Papi revealed when I asked him what he felt as I was getting married.

My wedding card had a poem that I had written as the invitation text. Papi used that poem in the beginning of his new book of poems translated in English by renowned poet Dr J.P. Das. The book titled *Autumn Moon* was published towards the end of 1999 and dedicated to Govind and me as a special wedding present.

By the time I returned from a delayed honeymoon in May 2000, it was almost as if the time for *Filhaal...* had finally come.

Papi was writing the lyrics for director Rakeysh Omprakash Mehra's supernatural thriller *Aks* which was being produced by Mr Jhamu Sughand. On the advice of my friend and colleague Sadhana, of Spectral Harmony studios, Papi mentioned my script to Jhamu*ji*. The following Monday I went over to his office to meet him. I handed my script over to Jhamu*ji* and left his office quite unsure of how the meeting had gone. I returned to his office two days later, wary, and he casually asked me, 'What cast have you thought of, for *our* film?' (So much like when Sippy saab had first asked Papi.)

Overwhelmed by all the pent-up emotion, I just broke down after okaying the first shot of *Filhaal* and Papi was there to cradle me … as always …

When I broke the news to Papi, it was almost as if a burden had been lifted off his chest. On the day of the mahurat, as soon as I okayed the first shot, I broke into tears in Papi's arms. Ma was crying too. But Papi was just plain relieved. His eyes were moist but he laughed and tried to make me laugh too. Papi says he had been feeling helpless as a father and would always be grateful to Jhamu*ji* for, as he says, 'Giving my daughter what I couldn't – her first film.'

Working with Papi on *Filhaal*… was a memorable experience – it was our first really professional interaction and Papi says I was very tough to please! There were times we didn't agree – but he always conceded to me, the director of the film, whose decision was final. There were scenes in which our perspectives differed and lyrics I rejected because they didn't match the mood I had in mind. He never once imposed his opinion on me, as a father or as film-maker – and a truly accomplished one at that.

When he commended me on seeing the first cut of *Filhaal*…, I took his praise with a pinch of salt. I know how much he adores

Music release of *Filhaal....*
It is very rare for Papi to be
at a loss for words, but on
the music release function
of *Filhaal...*, Papi choked
on his emotions as he
thanked Jhamu*ji* for giving
me what he couldn't – my
first film...

me. How could he possibly criticize me? It was only when Ma
saw the film and gave her approval that I breathed a little easier.

By the time *Filhaal...* was released in 2002, it was my turn
to goad Papi to make a film – it had been three years since *Hu
Tu Tu* had released. Not that he'd been sitting idle – his pen had
been scribbling away furiously on songs, screenplays and poems;
so much so that while writing this book it was quite a task to
keep track of all that he had done!

Imagine the magnitude of data I had to grapple with
when updating Papi's body of work for this new edition. I have
to admit that I've probably only scratched the surface of his
boundless creativity.

Papi says of any form of creativity – '*Karte ki vidya hai … karne se aati hei…*' (It is an applied talent, it comes only with application.) Papi still maintains the discipline of coming to his office every day, sitting and writing...

toot-ti neenden uthaana

jamaa karna khwaabon ke tukde

jo takiye se gire hon,

karvaton ki silvaton ko kholna

unko pirona.

jism ki kachchi daraaren dhoondna

toote phoote log le jaakar

sajaa leta hoon apne taaqchon mein

main kabaadi –

khaali dibbon botalon mein nazmein bharke bechta hoon…

Unpublished

as the page turns...

With *Hu Tu Tu* in 1999, a chapter closed for Papi – he did not want to direct films again. The experience of having his film distorted by the producers, who re-edited it, added a song and changed the background score – all without informing him – left a bitterness in his creative spirit.

It also opened up a hundred new chapters.

Papi's creativity found expression in many other forms – he has written songs for over fifty films in the past fifteen years, reinventing himself and his idiom with each film and lyric. '*Kajra Re*' (*Bunty aur Babli*), '*Namak*' (*Omkara*), '*Jai Ho*' (*Slumdog Millionaire*), '*Dil Toh Bachcha Hai Ji*' (*Ishqiya*), along with his songs for films like *Guru*, *Kaminey*, *Haider* and *Mirzya*, have exposed fresh layers of Papi's writing and lyrical expression.

Almost like an extension of his lyric-writing for films, Papi also collaborated with the choicest of musical talent like Ustad Amjad Ali Khan, Ustad Ghulam Ali, Sufi singer Abida Parveen, Rekha and Vishal Bhardwaj, and Bhupinder Singh on various non-film albums, including the distinguished *Gulzar in Conversation with Tagore* (2016), a collection of Tagore's poems and a song, translated and narrated by Papi, composed by Shantanu Moitra and sung by Shaan and Shreya Ghoshal.

Papi always says, 'There are more than a hundred books in my head!'

Those books found a release, and how! The last decade and a half has seen the writer and poet in him in overdrive. Papi could not be ruffled by the digitization of our world. For him – writing is still ink on paper, and the language remains Urdu.

With Farhana who has been invaluable with her work in transcribing all of Papi's writings ... she probably knows more about the volume of Papi's writing than anyone else.

For the first thirteen years of my life, Papi brought out a book on my birthday. It was a special moment for me to release one of his books – *Raat, Chaand aur Main* ... a collection of poems with the moon as the main theme.

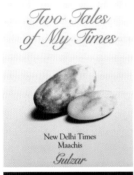

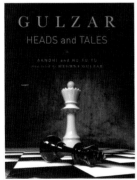

Keeping stride with him in as many years is Farhana, who meticulously transcribes all of Papi's writings into soft copy, both in Urdu and Hindi, when required. If anyone has a true tabulation of the entire scope of Papi's writings over the years, it is her.

In 2002, pocket-sized editions of Papi's collection of short stories, *Michelangelo and Other Stories* and *Seema and Other Stories*, as well as a compilation of his poems with references to Papi's favourite muse, the moon, called *Raat, Chaand aur Main*, were released. I had the privilege of releasing *Raat, Chaand aur Main*, at a function organized at Oxford Bookstore, Bombay.

Two Tales of My Times, the screenplays of two important films – *New Delhi Times* and *Maachis* – was published in 2008. Papi has been publishing his screenplays for years, and has devised an extremely reader-friendly format to present them. Translating the screenplays of *Aandhi* and *Hu Tu Tu* into English was *my* privilege and these were published in 2014 as *Heads & Tales*.

Along with several new collections of poems, short stories, children's books, lyrics and screenplays, Papi also took on the mammoth tasks of translating two iconic poets. He translated the

writings of eminent Marathi poet and writer, Kusumagraj. The book, *Kusumagraj ki Chuni Suni Nazmein*, was released in 2010. A symbiosis with the Marathi language was also born. Several of Papi's books were now being printed in Marathi, while Papi himself was translating the works of eminent Marathi writers. He is also a regular contributor to the Diwali issue of the Marathi magazine *Riturang*. His work with the Marathi language is facilitated by his dear friend and collaborator, Arun Shewte.

Another work of translation – a Herculean task in itself – was the translation of the works of Rabindranath Tagore. I had seen him at work on this pet project of his for years. It was initially planned as a project for Doordarshan, but they asked him to work on something on Munshi Premchand first. And so came about the serial *Tehreer Munshi Premchand Ki* which aired on Doordarshan in 2004 to much appreciation. In 2016, on the birth anniversary of Munshi Premchand, the screenplay editions of the serial were released, called *Godan, Nirmala and Other Stories*.

But Papi's ardent desire to do something with the works of Tagore persisted.

Papi has been closely involved with the stage and theatre over the last decade. Seen here with renowned theatre director Salim Arif and lyricist and singer Swananad Kirkire.

Kharaashein, a play based on Papi's writings about riots and emotional scarring, had one of its performances on Papi's birthday, 18 August 2002. Papi with close associate Salim Arif (seated second from right) and the *Kharaashein* team.

Papi had already begun dabbling in stage and theatre with renowned theatre director and close associate, Salim Arif. They had had several successful productions together based on Papi's writings.

In 2002, *Kharaashein* – a play based on Papi's short stories and poems about riots and the scars they leave on the human psyche – opened to audiences and was received with tremendous acclaim. It was followed by other successful productions like *Lakeerein*, based on Papi's writings on the Partition; *Atthaniyaan*, an exploration of a slice of life in Bombay; as well as comedies like *Chakkar Chalaaye Ghanchakkar* (based on *Angoor*) and productions for children like *Pinocchio*.

The 150th birth centenary of Rabindranath Tagore was coming up in 2011. As a tribute, Papi decided to translate one of Tagore's short stories, '*Streer Patra*' (A Wife's Letter), for the stage, to be directed by Salim-bhai.

Translating Tagore gave Papi a sense of fulfilment – he had been introduced to Tagore through the Urdu translation of Tagore's book of poems, *The Gardener*. It is what had made him

Papi's longstanding dream of translating Tagore came true in 2016 with the release of a twin set of books, *Gulzar Translates Tagore*. The first copy of the book was unveiled by and gifted to our then President, Shri Pranab Mukherjee.

turn from reading jasoosi novels towards serious literature. And he never returned the borrowed book to the lending library.

Most regional-language translations of Tagore have come from English. Papi translated his work directly from Bengali. And decisively picked writings from when Tagore was younger; writings in which you see a young, romantic poet instead of the profound, older auteur whose works we are more familiar with.

Papi's tribute to the work of Rabindranath Tagore was released in the form of a twin set of books in 2016. *Gulzar Translates Tagore* consisted of *Baaghbaan*, a translation of Tagore's poems curated from collections such as *Chitra*, *Kshanika* and *Sonar Tari*; and *Nindiya Chor*, which had translations from *Shishu*, a collection of poems giving Tagore's insights into the world of a child. The first copy of *Gulzar Translates Tagore* was gifted to our then President, Shri Pranab Mukherjee, at Rashtrapati Bhavan, New Delhi.

With *Gulzar Translates Tagore* it was as if he had completed a circle.

The Rabindra Bharati University, Kolkata, also conferred an honorary Doctor of Letters to Papi at its fortieth annual convocation on 8 May 2015.

Papi being conferred an honorary Doctor of Letters by the Rabindra Bharati University.

The year 2017 was one of many special 'firsts'.

Continuing with his love for all things Bengali, Papi's first books were published in the Bengali language. One was a translation of his book of poems, *Pluto*. The second was a compilation of essays about his interactions with Bengalis in his career as a film-maker and litterateur. As is Papi's penchant with interesting titles, *Panta Bhate* (which refers to cooked leftover rice kept in water overnight, and is considered a delicacy) encapsulated Papi's experiences with his mentor Bimal Roy, with Hemant Kumar and S.D. Burman, along with his memories of Samaresh Basu, Satyajit Ray and R.D. Burman, among others. Interestingly enough, despite his close to seventy-year-old tryst with Bengali, it was only in 2017 that his first books in the language were published. Another volume, a translation of *Suspected Poems*, is scheduled for August 2018.

Also in 2017, Papi accomplished two more 'firsts'.

His first novel, *Do Log*, was published in Hindi. Its English translation is titled *Two*. It has been translated from Hindi by Papi himself, his first time as translator!

Footprints on Zero Line – a collection of Papi's writings on the Partition – including fiction, non-fiction and poems was also

published in 2017. He says that it is only now, with these books, that he has finally been able to purge the scars of the Partition.

Whatever else he is writing, Papi's writing for children remains incessant. His association with various children's organizations has remained. Papi has been closely associated with Arushi, a non-profit organization for persons

Papi's involvement with children continues through his various books for children and his association with Arushi, a non-profit organization for persons with disabilities.

with disabilities, in Bhopal, for over twenty-five years now. Anil Mudgal and Prof. Rohit of Arushi are close associates who have been working with Papi on various books for children and other events over the years.

Appreciation and recognition for his works have remained concurrent throughout Papi's career, be it as a film-maker, or as a litterateur and poet. In 2001, Papi was awarded the honorary lifetime fellowship at the Indian Institute of Advanced Study. His tally of Filmfare trophies now stands at twenty with the lifetime achievement award in 2002. He has won the prestigious National Award seven times – best screenplay for *Koshish*, best director for

At the staging of his translation of *The Adventures of Pinocchio*.

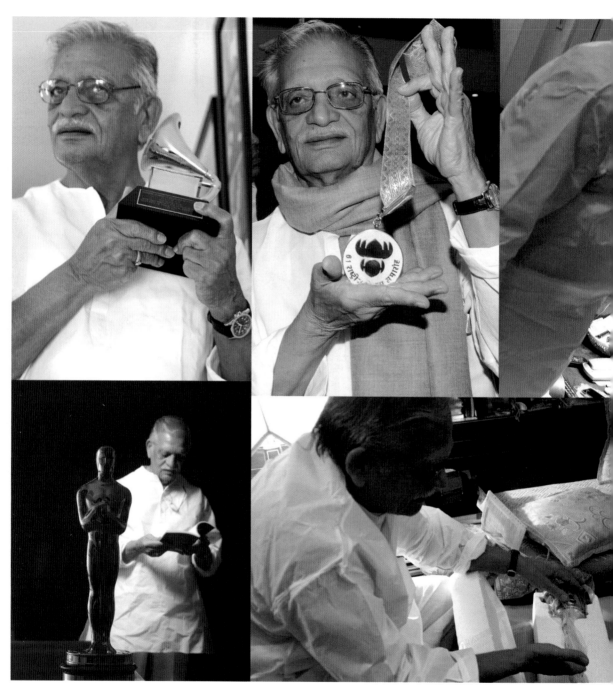

It has been raining awards for Papi over the last few years. He was conferred the Dadasaheb Phalke Award in 2013. His tally of Filmfare Awards now stands at twenty. He won the Sahitya Akademi Award for *Dhuaan* in 2003. In 2009, came the Academy Award for Best Original Song for '*Jai Ho*', which also won the Grammy Award for Best Song Written for a Motion Picture, Television or Other Visual Media.

Mausam and best lyricist for *Ijaazat* and *Lekin*. *Maachis* won the National Award for best film providing wholesome entertainment while his documentaries on Pandit Bhimsen Joshi and Ustad Amjad Ali Khan won the award for best documentary.

His book of children's stories, *Ekta*, received an award from NCERT. Dearly cherished is the Sahitya Akademi Award he got in January 2003 for *Dhuaan*, his collection of Urdu short stories. In 2004, Papi was awarded the Padma Bhushan, the third-highest civilian award in India, for his contribution to the arts. He was conferred the Dadasaheb Phalke Award – the highest award in Indian cinema – in 2013. He has now been honoured with every top award one could win for cinema, art and literature in India. And there was international acclaim as well.

In 2009, Papi won the Academy Award for Best Original Song as lyricist for the song '*Jai Ho*' from the film *Slumdog Millionaire*. The same song also went on to win the Grammy Award in 2010, for Best Song Written for a Motion Picture, Television or Other Visual Media. Papi shared the award as lyricist with music director A.R. Rahman and playback singer Tanvi Shah.

He did not go for the Oscars. Neither for the Grammys.

He is often asked, 'Why?'

He replies with characteristic humour that he doesn't have the customary 'black tuxedo' that one is expected to wear at the Academy Awards. In truth, Papi had a muscle injury on his shoulder and was advised against travel.

But he had a far more pressing reason for missing the Grammys in 2010.

He was about to become a grandfather…

samandar dekh raha tha
samandar se, meri amrit ki kumbhi aane waali thi
samandar karvatein leta tha, reh reh kar, toh bal padte thay paani mein
meri bachchi ki naazuk kokh se teesein guzarti theen
mujhe uss waqt dar lagta tha, amrit maangne se.

usey jab kapkapi aati thi toh main kaanp jaata tha
woh pyaasi thi —
magar paani mana tha,
barf ki daliyaan phiraayi jaa rahi theen khushk hoton par
samandar apne paani mein hi ghotey khaane lagta tha
samandar kaat ke 'kumbhi' nikalo
na kaatoge toh marr jaaegi bachchi.

mere 'amrit ki kumbhi' ko woh jab godi mein lekar ab khilati hai
mere andar se koi mard kehta hai,
'tumhein taufeeq hi na thi,
ki tum ye dard sehte aur ik insaan ki takhleeq karte!'

'*Meghna*': NEGLECTED POEMS

creating circles,
completing circles…

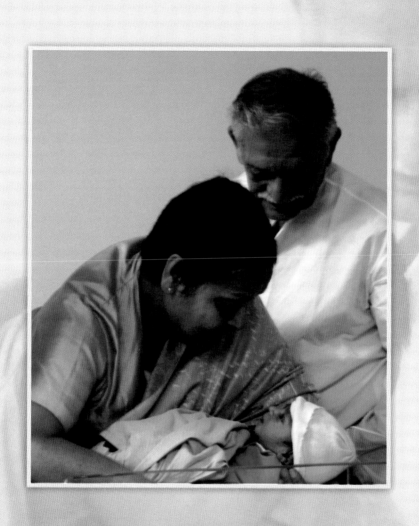

'Pram-ing' it with Nanoo.

I went into labour in the wee hours of 8 February 2010. It was an excruciating fourteen-hour wait before I was ushered into the delivery room, for what eventually ended up being a caesarean delivery. There were two worried mothers at the hospital – Ma and Geeta mama, my mother-in-law. (I was too preoccupied with dealing with the contractions, to be worried.)

Also, there were two worried fathers.

Govind, my boyfriend who became my husband, was now becoming a father. And my father, my Papi, was going to be Nanoo.

Everything about our world, our lives as we knew it, was to change from that day on. And as Samay's father, it is both poignant and pertinent to have Govind's insights too in this chapter.

Always worried but never showing it – that is Nanoo.

His presence has always been reassuring; as it was that day for me, the worried father. We make for an interesting combination in worrisome times – I totally shut down to clinically focus on the task at hand; and he is so aware of other people's emotions that he keeps quiet and soaks them in. Either way there isn't much conversation except reassuring looks being exchanged.

Samay with Nani.

After a week's stay in the hospital, Samay and I came home. Then followed the mandatory forty-day period of being confined to the house. Just like when I was young, Papi now realigned his workday for Samay's routine.

We celebrated the end of the forty-day confinement with a trip to the gurudwara and a havan at home. Now the world was waiting to unfold like an adventure.

In a household full of activity, two mothers instructing the new mother, the new mother learning, fighting, crying, the nanny acting up – and

Samay's first day at preschool.

in the midst of many more chaotic, new, fun things — there was always Nanoo as the constant. Never saying much to any of the actors involved, only doing his bit of being around with a comforting presence.

At the stroke of five every evening, Nanoo was there to take Samay for a drive. (Papi's penchant for punctuality is well-known. Samay now realizes he can tell the time by when Nanoo arrives!)

Papi realized that this one hour and some, each evening, was a very crucial relief for a young mother; and this ritual of being with him every evening carried on for the first five years of Samay's life.

When Samay got a few months older, the drives turned into walks, with Samay in a pram. The pram strolls turned into crawls and stumblings in the sand pits of Joggers' Park, Bandra; and the stumblings turned into little walks. Through each step, Nanoo always showed up as promised and when he promised.

On Samay's first day at preschool, separation anxiety hit the grandparents more than the parents! In the initial days, I would

With Nani and Nanoo at Samay's playschool, The Little Company, Bandra.

Papi's mojris continue to fascinate Samay's classmates as they did mine.

wait outside his classroom, as instructed by the teachers, in case Samay would have difficulty adjusting. Both Papi and Ma took turns accompanying me in my wait. Again, like when I was in school, both Papi and Ma were there together, to attend functions at Samay's playschool. The Little Company, Bandra, was a wonderful learning environment where Samay blossomed under the care of Miss Marzia and Miss Harjit Kaur. On one occasion, Papi was invited for a storytelling session with the children. I can't be sure who enjoyed it more – the children, the teachers or Papi himself! But what happened at the end of the session stayed with me.

As Papi was coming out of the classroom to put on his mojris, the children followed, to put on their shoes. And then they caught sight of the fascinating golden twirl at the top of Papi's mojris and began to reach out and touch it. 'What is this?', 'Are you a king?', 'Why does your shoe have a moustache?' The questions were endearing … and endless. That moment took me right back to when I was in school, and there was Papi with his mojris, among my awestruck schoolmates!

Samay's first Holi.

As a child, Samay would be very averse to touching anything wet and mushy. In preschool, he would stay away from any kind of finger-painting activities. We realized that the best way to help him overcome this aversion was to douse ourselves, and him, with colour! So, when Samay turned two, our celebration of Holi started again.

It is ironic that Nanoo too loves Holi and would always have people over to celebrate Holi at his bungalow. Now, that tradition has been passed onto Samay. Samay loves his Holi. For him, Holi begins with marching to Nanoo's bungalow and painting Nanoo in all the

Just like he did with me, Papi has got Samay his own canvases to paint.

colours available! Samay's friends come over and it is a delight to see a gathering which ranges from seven to eighty years in age, with Nanoo playing host to his own friends, his daughter's friends and being bullied by seven-year-olds.

Papi's bungalow is a haven for Samay and a sanctuary for his toys. What used to be my room there is now his. Samay's scribblings are now on the walls where once mine used to be. And just like he did with me, Papi got Samay his own canvases to paint alongside him.

Samay has also inherited his love for nature from his grandparents. The idyllic days spent with the entire family at Nani's farm among cows, rabbits, dogs and chickens has enriched Samay's childhood immensely. That Govind has also provided a similar environment for Samay at our farm in Karjat – about two hours away from Mumbai – is something that comforts Papi immensely. Consequently, Samay now has a keen interest as well as knowledge about animals, marine life, nature and all kinds of critters that abound in it. He and Nani can spend hours chatting on the subject.

Nani and Nanoo have inculcated in Samay a love for nature.

With the coming of Samay, the festival of Holi too has come back to our home with a splash.

Samay has come to understand his grandparents' roles very well.

They are always there.

Nanoo can be taken for shopping without complaining. Nani is always there when Samay returns from school. Nanoo delivers the candy – whenever they meet, Samay will frisk Nanoo to look for that secret Fox candy which Nanoo will have somewhere on him. As a reinforcement, there is Nani as well, with some chocolate hidden in the depths of her handbag. Her other specialty is feeding him his favourite fish fingers.

Both Nanoo and Nani can be used on special occasions to get Mom and Dad scolded, to align with his agenda – Nanoo is supportive of the oppressed without offending the dictators. Last but definitely not the least, Nanoo has even facilitated a zoo in his bungalow. Throughout Samay's growing-up years, Nanoo has learnt to keep fish, parrots, rabbits, a dog that was adopted from Carter Road and many others. This particular generosity was innocently exploited to the point where we had to have our own farm and spare Nanoo of all the livestock trouble.

As Samay has grown, so have we as a family; and I can see the contours of our relationships evolving. I think Nanoo's anchor has enabled Samay to have a deep-rooted sense of family that you can only have if you see the layers of your family together.

By the time Samay was around three, Papi began to wonder about my career … when would I go back to making films? It had been over six years since my last film had released. And he shared his concerns with Vishal.

Papi and Vishal share a rare bond. Professionally, they know each other's pulse and that is evident in all their collaborations. No one can get Papi to write like Vishal does. Papi feels Vishal understands his poetry better than anyone else. It is no surprise then that almost all of Vishal's compositions have Papi's words.

When their lines between the personal and the professional blurred is also blurry in my memory. Vishal is like an elder son to Papi and holds Papi in the highest regard, like a father. They reach out to each other for advice, to share a concern, or even just to unburden the mind. So, it was only natural that both Papi and Vishal began talking to me about my next film. And it is only because of Vishal that *Talvar* happened to me.

Making a film meant time away from home, and from Samay. And I was blessed that my entire family – Papi, Ma, Geeta mama (my mother-in-law), my sister-in-law Rajita and more than anyone, Govind – rallied together to ensure that my absence would not affect Samay adversely. When my absences became too long, Papi, Govind and Samay flew to Delhi to be with me while I was shooting. Samay visited me in Kashmir too, while I was shooting for my film *Raazi*. Just like I would visit Papi's sets when I was a child.

And so it has been since…

Just like I would visit Papi's sets when I was a child, Samay visits me on my outdoor shoots.

Top: On the sets of *Raazi.*
Bottom: On the sets of *Talvar*

This year, 2018, as Samay turned eight, Nanoo gifted him a book – *Samay ka Khatola* – a collection of poems, stories and songs for children, with the first poem dedicated to him. Much like he had done each year on my birthday, for my first thirteen years.

Papi had completed yet another circle, and begun a new one…

chhota sa 'planet' samjha tha, paida hua hai
mere 'solar system' mein!
mera navaasa — mera Samay!

do hi saal ka hai aur yun mehsoos hota hai
sooraj woh hai aur hum sab —
uske 'planet' hain,
uske gird ghooma karte hain
moh mein kaisi 'gravity' jaisi taaqat hoti hai!

'Samay': SAMAY KA KHATOLA

déjà vu…

A family that eats together stays together. Papi, Ma, Govind, Samay and I often go out for dinner to our favourite suburban restaurants. We make it a point to have at least a couple of meals a month together.

T he more things change, the more they remain the same…

It is almost 11 p.m. Papi, Ma, Govind, Samay and I have just finished dinner at our favourite restaurant. We catch up on what each of us is doing presently – Ma's new cultivations at her farm, Govind's impending business trip, the progress on my current film, Samay's day in school and the dozens of books that Papi is reading and writing simultaneously.

The conversation veers towards us taking a vacation together. We haven't had one as a family in the last few years.

As a tradition, Papi had decided to take us to one historical place every year on his birthday. His motivation being that we were less likely to visit these places on our own, but that these are places in our country we must see. In keeping with this, we had visited the Ajanta and Ellora caves, and made a trip to Mandu to see the palaces of Baz Bahadur and Rani Roopmati. There, Papi narrated their fables in his own inimitable style, sprinkling them with generous doses of his imagination. On that trip we visited the Sanchi stupas as well.

Papi, Govind and I taking in the view from Princess Roopmati's palace, Mandu.

Weaving fables against the backdrop of the famous Jahaaz Mahal, Mandu. Some history ... some imagination!

Papi was very excited to be in Mandu with us because he had shot for *Kinaara* there, and everywhere we went, the local people still seemed to remember that he had! The entire trip had been meticulously planned and arranged with the help of Farokhbhai, who had also accompanied us along with his nephew Balu.

The other favourite family destination is the Kumarakom Lake resort in Kerala. We went there for the first time in 2009, on Papi's seventy-fifth birthday. Papi's dear friend Brij Bakshi also joined us for a couple of days for the special occasion. It is a beautiful lakeside retreat, owned by the warm and gracious Paul John. He too joined us for Papi's birthday, along with his close friend Ali. As a family, we love the place so much that we promptly returned in 2011, and again in 2013.

We haven't been back to Kerala for the last few years. In fact, a vacation together for all of us is long overdue. I haven't been able to get away as I have been either shooting a film or engaged in its post-production. And thankfully, no one is really

Kerala, particularly the Kumarakom Lake resort, is a favourite holiday destination for the family. We visited it in 2011 and 2013.

On the sets of *Talvar*.

complaining. Both Ma and Papi have been concerned about my career for years. All parents want their child to do well. And here I was — my first film had met with critical acclaim but commercial success had been eluding me ever since I began making films. If my struggles were difficult for me, it was that much more for Papi and Ma — they could only watch silently. Fortunately, things changed for the better with *Talvar*. And more than being happy about its success, I was relieved that finally, at least now, I may have eased some of my parents' worries.

Adding to the critical and commercial success of *Talvar* was the acquittal of Rajesh and Nupur Talwar, of all charges of murdering their daughter Aarushi and their household help Hemraj, by the Hon'ble Allahabad High Court.

As a film-maker, that was my gratification. The verdict was an affirmation of everything I had felt — from the time I was collating the research material for the film, and through the making of it.

My award was the poem that Papi wrote for me. It remains unpublished, but I am sharing it here…

kai barson se seene mein rakha tha aasmaan…

kai barson se seene mein rakha tha aasmaan tay karke maine
meri ummeedon ke naqshe thay uss par,
mere khwaabon ke baadal thay,
mere ashkon ka paani tha!

main nanhi ungliyaan beti ki sehlata tha, unko choomta tha
badi ho kar ye mera aasmaan kholegi ik din
woh apna kehkashaan uss par bichhaaegi!

badi ho kar meri beti ne khola aasmaan aur,
ungliyon se naam apna likh ke roshan kar diya hai aasmaan mera

kai barson se jo tay karke maine seene mein rakha hua tha!

Unpublished

On the sets of *Raazi*.

The success of *Raazi* has doubled Papi's sense of contentment. The word 'tasalli' was often heard in our household as the film was being loved both critically and commercially. The songs of *Raazi*, with their simple, old-world emotions, have also struck a chord with the listeners, and in keeping with tradition, I have made Papi rewrite one of the songs of the film, a couple of times!

He rues that I hardly ever share my script with him while it is being written; I only show it to him after it is complete. And the same goes for the film as well. Papi barely visits my film set once or at the most twice.

I am perhaps the least favourite of Papi's directors – Vishal, Shaad Ali and Rakeysh Omprakash Mehra being the more favoured. He says, by virtue of being his daughter, I take undue advantage of him, which the others don't do. This is something I vehemently disagree with. I have mentioned before – no one extracts out of Papi what Vishal does. In fact, Rakeysh even managed to coax Papi into writing his film *Mirzya*, which Papi rarely does, as he feels it takes away too much time from his other literary writings.

Celebrating Holi with his favourite directors, Vishal and Rakeysh.

Apart from *Raazi*, Papi has on his slate this year Vishal's next film *Patakha*, Shaad's film *Soorma* and Rakeysh's *Mere Pyaare Prime Minister*. Along with these film-makers, music composers Shankar-Ehsaan-Loy are Papi's favourites as well. Apart from Vishal, Papi has worked the most with them. When they came on board

At the music recording of *Raazi*. Papi was so in sync with the three composers Shankar-Ehsaan-Loy that I felt like an intruder!

to do the music for *Raazi*, Papi was so in sync with the three of them that I felt like an intruder!

On the literary front, there are still several more books in Papi's head; and in the pipeline as well. Another passion project that he is working on is tentatively titled *A Poem a Day*. Papi is translating 365 poems by over 250 contemporary poets from thirty-two different languages and dialects of the Indian subcontinent. These include the writings of Indian poets writing in English, Urdu, Hindi and other regional languages and little-known dialects of the country, as well as poems from countries like Nepal, Sri Lanka, Bangladesh and Pakistan.

Papi plays three sets of tennis a day and 'often beats men half his age'. When this line appeared in print in an interview, his friends from the gymkhana asked him, 'Who are these men you beat?' They didn't mind being called half his age though!

In spite of all of us now having busy days, as a family we make it a point to have dinner together at least a couple of times a month, when we share all that is going on with each of us. We try and finish these

Papi keenly observes the progress of Govind's beautification project for his garden. The arrival of sparrows, other birds, and even the tiniest buds that bloom delight him!

Papi with our driver of almost thirty years, Sundar. It's uncanny, the longevity of all of Papi's associations and relationships...

family dinners early, as Papi wakes up very early in the mornings. Tonight, we have managed to leave the restaurant by 11 p.m. and Papi says he will make it for his tennis game tomorrow morning. And he does…

Papi wakes up by 5:00 a.m. Thrice a week, he does yoga along with our shared teacher, Yatin Dave. By 6:00 a.m. he is on the tennis court at Bandra Gymkhana. Some days he plays a few games, some days it's just knocking the ball for some time, along with a walk. The Gymkhana is probably the only place Sundar does not drive Papi to. All other destinations are reached with his able driving – Sundar has been with us for over forty years now! In fact, it was Sundar who taught *me* how to drive too.

Papi's regular companion to the Bandra Gymkhana is Umesh Pachigar. Just like Dr Hussain Taylor used to be. They go to the Gymkhana together, either play or take a walk together, before Papi comes home around 8 a.m. Interestingly, even at eighty-four, Papi is still playing in the Gymkhana tournament, and winning too!

Once home, a cup of tea is mandatory as Papi reads the morning paper, in the study or in the balcony if he is getting shaved by Atiullah. Actually, Papi prefers to drink tea in a tall glass, not in a cup. That's how he likes his whiskey too. Along with tea, Papi munches on some biscuits, coconut or 'shrews berry', which were once shared with Pali as well.

Dressed in his trademark crisp white kurta and white pants (not pyjamas, as is largely believed), and his golden mojris, Papi comes downstairs to his office at about 10.30 a.m. There, he is met by Farhana and his office manager. Till I moved into Cozihom after my marriage, Papi used to have his office there. Since then, the lower floor of his bungalow, 'Boskyana', has been converted into

For years, Papi has worn this kind of golden mojri with an upturned chonch (beak). He used to wear them when he travelled abroad too, but switched to sneakers when he realized they attract too much attention; little girls would come and touch the chonch in amusement!

the office. He had donated one of the rooms for my office as well, but instead, Govind works out of there sometimes.

After going over the day's mail and other correspondence that is to be addressed, Papi gets down to writing – a poem that he is translating, or one he is creating anew, or a song that he is writing for somebody or an article that he is contributing to some publication. When I was writing this book, thirteen years ago, and putting the finishing touches to it, I used to wonder, how am I going to end it? Papi, everything he is and does, is, well, ceaseless! And the more things change, the more they remain the same.

Papi has a few meetings, incessant phone calls and a few 'glasses' of tea. To avoid having excessive tea during the day, Papi has come up with a concoction called *kaala paani* – hot water with lime juice, honey and rock salt. It's just as stimulating, without the harmful effects of tea.

Papi has added another stroke to his creative repertoire – he had always painted – oil on canvas. A few years ago, he began to dabble with watercolours. And now he is exploring charcoal as a medium. In fact, a few of his sketches have been published in his recent books, *Pluto* (a collection of poems), *Footprints on Zero Line: Writings on the Partition* and his novel *Two* (Do Log).

If it is a school holiday, it is assured that Samay will barge into the bungalow to play in his room there. But not before disrupting Nanoo's work a little bit. Suffice it to say, Papi adores the interruption. Samay will sit on his chair, put on his glasses and pretend to write like Nanoo does. Or he may want to take some candles out of Papi's collection and play with them.

Papi has been collecting candles for years – all shapes and sizes and kinds. I would often tease him about lighting a few on Diwali and he would retort as he always does – '*Maar daloonga!*' (I'll kill you!)

Papi has an enviable collection of Buddha heads. He collects candles, driftwood and shells too. This is my favourite from all of Papi's Buddha heads – its serene expression is very soothing.

Papi also has an amazing collection of Buddha's heads – in stone, wood, coral, jade, terracotta, etc. Some are even replicas of antique sculptures from ancient times. Each head is given a place in the stone wall of the living room which has ledges and niches. My favourite is the huge wooden Buddha head that sits in his bedroom. The serene expression on its face is very soothing.

If Samay hasn't visited Papi's bungalow for a few days, Papi will come over to see Samay in the evening. As Samay got older and began karate and basketball classes, the drives and walks with Nanoo changed to Nanoo accompanying Samay to his classes. Papi sits patiently till Samay's class comes to an end, then brings him home. Most evenings, Ma is also there at our house, waiting for Samay to return.

As a family, we had decided that Samay would never be home without a family member around while I was away making my films. So, both Papi and Ma make it a point to be there for him.

Interestingly, Papi never comes to my house empty-handed. Even if it is a casual visit. Perhaps it has something to do with

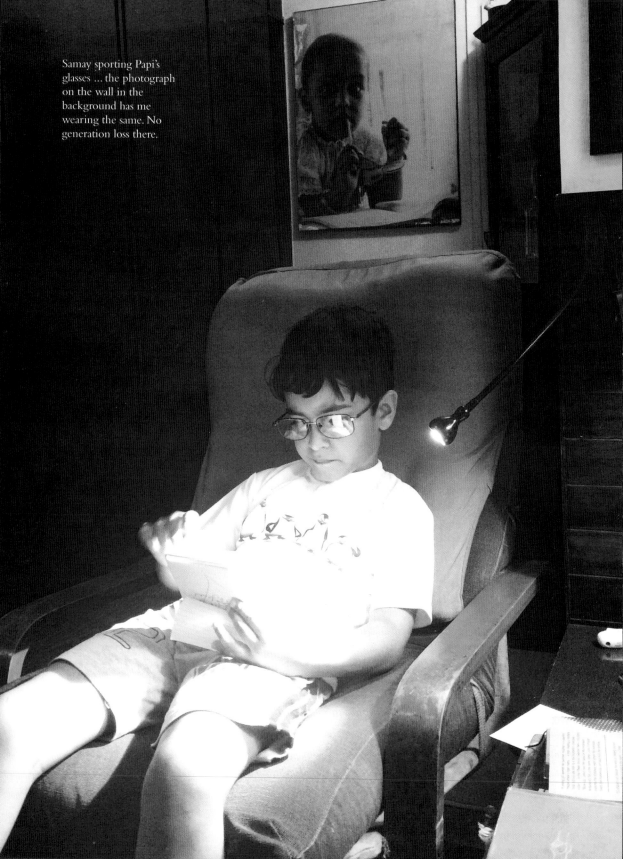

Samay sporting Papi's glasses ... the photograph on the wall in the background has me wearing the same. No generation loss there.

the tradition of not taking anything from your daughter's marital home, but Papi will always carry something each time he comes – even if it is fruit! Papi goes to the local fruit-seller at least a couple of times a month to buy fruit. And then asks us every day if we have eaten the fruit, had the juice…

This time Papi has some Lucknawi salwar kurtas he has brought for Ma and me from one of his trips. He and Ma agree to barter – salwar kurtas in exchange for *Ileesh maachher jhol* and *shorshe baata chingdi maachh* (Hilsa fish curry and prawns in mustard). The exchange shall take place on the coming weekend at my house. Ma says she will include mutton chops for Govind. As is common knowledge, Ma loves to cook and Govind really does justice to her cooking.

Papi loves this picture of me comfortable in his chair … taken just before I was married.

Once back home, Papi settles into his favourite chair in the bedroom that Ma had gifted him, and picks up the book he is currently reading. Actually, he reads about three books at a time and puts them on the shelves only after he has finished reading them. So, his sitting area, as also his working desk, is constantly submerged under piles of books. He may spend some time on his iPad,

Papi got initiated into computers about seven years ago. Today, he corresponds extensively on email, surfs the internet – his favourite website being NASA, and even has his scripts on the computer – in Urdu!

reading or watching something. Papi's initiation to the iPad and his familiarity with it has been under the able tutelage of Samay! Samay even has his own games and apps downloaded on Papi's device, much to his continued amazement.

Unless someone drops in for a drink or dinner, Papi watches television for the nightly news. Sometimes he may have a drink, relaxing in his quiet solitude and then sits for dinner by 8:30 p.m. Papi has a tremendous sweet tooth; he says he goes through the entire meal just so he can get dessert! He relishes kulfi, rabdi, or any Bengali sweet. If there's no preferred dessert at home (which is very unlikely), he settles for a piece of gud.

But for very special exceptions, it is generally lights-out by 10 p.m. Papi says, Ma had told him once, '*Agar aap shaayar na hote, toh bade hi ordinary hote!*' (If you weren't a poet, you would be a very ordinary man!) Papi has even used this line in *Aandhi* – with Suchitra Sen making the remark at Sanjeev Kumar.

So, his seemingly mundane day comes to an end.

Till he beats the sun at sunrise again the next day.

And weaves a whole new day with his words, his songs, his poems and his scripts … with his simple gestures of concern and affection … in his pensive moments and his smiles … being a poet, a writer, a film-maker, a friend, a husband, a father, a grandfather … and so much more … always.

woh kya hai, jo 'kuchh' pighalta rehta hai mere andar
ubharta rehta hai jism par qatra qatra! kya hai?
gharon ki kuchh kacchi-kacchi deevarein mitti ki,
maine dekhi hain pehle baarishon mein
meenh barasta hai unn gharon par,
toh risne lagti hai mitti unki
woh kya hai jo 'kuchh' barasta rehta hai mere andar!

suraahiyaan maine dekhi hain garmiyon mein aksar
bhari rahein toh woh risne lagti hain qatra qatra
woh kya hai jo 'kuchh' bhara hai aur ris raha hai andar?

ubalte paani ki degchi par,
paseene ki boondein ban-ne lagti hain, dekhta hoon
ke bhaap uthti hai, khad-khadata hai uska dhakkan
toh bajne lagti hain, mere andar ki pasliyaan bhi
woh 'kuchh' toh hai jo ubalta rehta hai mere andar
woh 'kuchh' toh hai jo pighalta rehta hai mere andar
jo qatra qatra pighalta hai aur main kaagazon par sambhaalta hoon!

'*Woh kya hai*': UNPUBLISHED

papi's word now...

I wish my mirror could retain my images from the past. So that I could see how I looked then. It is not only the looks, but also how I behaved.

My daughter Bosky has done that in the new edition of her book *Because He Is*. She is my mirror. She has the opportunity to improve my behaviour and mend my mistakes – by ignoring them. But I know she is too honest and straightforward. I respect her honesty. I always do. The presence of Govind, my son-in-law, is 'sone par suhaaga'. He understands my weaknesses and doesn't mind pouring a Patiala Peg for me.

It is a great transition when your children become your guardians. Even my little one, my grandson, only eight years old, tells me while playing cricket: '*Nanoo, aap baithh jaao, thak jaaoge*!' He is Samay.

Bosky is Meghna now.

She has grown into a full-fledged writer and director. She makes her films with complete conviction and social responsibility. She is a better film-maker than I was, in cinematic terms and social consciousness. She thinks I am biased. I agree with that too.

It is so fulfilling to see her success after a long struggle. I have watched her go through heaps of files when she was researching and working on *Talvar*. I could not give her a launch like most film-makers have for their children. Perhaps she had it tougher, being the daughter of well-known parents.

I love my threesome family of Govind, Meghna (Bosky) and Samay. Raakhee and myself are fortunate to play the role of Nanoo and Nani. Raakhee is still a disciplinarian, I am still a 'bachcha bigadoo'. I am reliving my former role of a father, as grandfather now.

It's too late for me to change.

I remain as I was.

Gulzar
'2018.

some important

milestones…

Films

Mere Apne	(1971)
Parichay	(1972)
Koshish	(1972)
Achaanak	(1973)
Khushboo	(1974)
Aandhi	(1975)
Mausam	(1976)
Kinaara	(1977)
Kitaab	(1978)
Angoor	(1980)
Namkeen	(1981)
Meera	(1981)
Ijaazat	(1986)
Mirza Ghalib (TV Serial & Music Album)	(1988)
Lekin…	(1990)
Ustad Amjad Ali Khan (Documentary)	(1990)
Pt. Bhimsen Joshi (Documentary)	(1992)
Libaas	(1993, Unreleased)
Kirdaar (TV Serial)	(1993)
Maachis	(1996)
Hu Tu Tu	(1999)
Tehreer Munshi Premchand Ki (TV Serial)	(2004)

Non-film music albums

Dil Padosi Hai, (with R.D. Burman and Asha Bhosle), 1987

Boodhe Pahaadon Par, (with Vishal and Suresh Wadkar), 1997

Maraasim, (with Jagjit Singh), 1999

Vaada, (with Ustad Amjad Ali Khan), 1999

Sunset Point, (with Bhupinder, Chitra and Vishal), 2000

Visaal, (with Ghulam Ali), 2001

Main Aur Mera Saaya, (with Bhupen Hazarika), 1992

Udaas Paani, (with Abhishek Ray), 2002

Ishqa Ishqa, (with Rekha and Vishal Bhardwaj), 2002

Abida Sings Kabir, (with Abida Parveen), 2003

Koi Baat Chale, (with Jagjit Singh), 2006

Chaand Parosa Hai, (with Bhupinder Singh), 2008

Barse Barse, (with Vishal and Suresh Wadkar), 2011

Aksar, (with Bhupinder and Mitali), 2012

Surmayi Raat, (with Bhupinder Singh), 2013

Gulzar in Conversation with Tagore, (with Shantanu Moitra, Shaan and Shreya Ghoshal), 2016

Tapur Tupur: Tagore's Poems for Children, (with Shantanu Moitra), 2016

Books

Chauras Raat, (Short stories), 1962

Jaanam, (Poems), 1963

Ek Boond Chaand, (Poems), 1972

Kuchh Aur Nazmein, (Poems), 1980

Dastakhat, (Urdu Poems, published in Pakistan), 1989

Pukhraj, (Poems translated in English), 1994

Silences, (Poems translated in English), 1994

Raavi Paar, (Short stories, editions in English and other languages), 1997

Autumn Moon, (Poems translated in English), 1999

Kaayda, (Hindi alphabets in verse for children), 2000

Triveni, (Poems translated in Hindi), 2001

Ek Mein Do, (Scholastic book for children), 2001

Raat Pashmine Ki, (Poems, Urdu and Hindi editions), 2002

Michelangelo & Other Stories, (Short stories, English translation), 2002

Seema & Other Stories, (Short stories, English translation), 2002

Habu Ki Aag & Other Stories, (Short stories, English translation), 2002

Addha & Other Stories, (Short stories, English translation), 2002

Khauff & Other Stories, (Short stories, English translation), 2002

Splinter & Other Poems, (Poems translated in English), 2002

Raat, Chaand Aur Main, (Poems translated in English), 2002

Ek Ghar Naam Saal, (Scholastic book for children), 2003

Meera, (Screenplay), 2004

Parwaaz: Autobiography of A.P.J. Abdul Kalam, (Audio-book, Hindi Translation and Narration), 2004

Selected Poems, (Poems translated in English), 2008

Two Tales of My Times, (Screenplays of *New Delhi Times* and *Maachis,* English translation), 2008

100 Lyrics, (Selection of lyrics, Hindi with English translation), 2009

Kusumagraj Ki Gini Suni Nazmein, (Translation), 2010

Magical Wishes: The Adventures of Goopy and Bagha, (Scholastic book for children), 2010

Mirza Ghalib: A Biographical Scenario, 2011

Neglected Poems, (Poems translated in English), 2012

My Favourite Stories: Bosky's Panchatantra, 2013

Half A Rupee: Stories, (Short stories, English translation), 2013

Meelo Se Din, (Selected Film Songs), 2013

Heads & Tales, (Screenplays of *Aandhi* and *Hu Tu Tu,* English Translation), 2014

Green Poems, (Poems, Hindi and English Translation), 2014

Pluto, (Poems, Hindi and English Translation), 2015

Gulzar Translates Tagore:

Baaghbaan and *Nindiya Chor,* (Translation), 2016

Godan, Nirmala and Other Stories, (Screenplay), 2016

Another 100 Lyrics, (Selection of lyrics, Hindi with English Translation), 2016

Suspected Poems, (Poems translated in English), 2017

Do Log, (A Novel, Hindi), 2017

Two, (A Novel, English), 2017

Footprints on Zero Line, (Writings on the Partition), 2017

Pluto, (Poems in Bengali translation), 2017

Panta Bhate, (Essays in Bengali), 2017

Gulzar Patkatha, (Screenplays in Marathi), 2017

Samay Ka Khatola, (Collection of Poems, Stories and Songs for Children), 2018

Some Significant Others...

Bandini, 'Mora gora ang lai le', Lyrics, 1963

Khamoshi, Lyrics, 1969

Aashirvaad, Screenplay, Dialogue and Lyrics, 1969

Guddi, Story, Screenplay, Dialogue and Lyrics, 1971

Seema, Lyrics, 1971

Namak Haram, Dialogue and Lyrics, 1972

Anand, Dialogue and Lyrics, 1973

Ghar, Dialogue and Lyrics, 1977

Gharonda, Lyrics, 1978

Gol Maal, Lyrics, 1979

Griha Pravesh, Dialogue and Lyrics, 1979

Khoobsurat, Dialogue and Lyrics, 1980

Thodi Si Bewafaai, Lyrics, 1980

Sitara, Screenplay, Dialogue and Lyrics, 1980

Baseraa, Dialogue and Lyrics, 1981

Masoom, Screenplay, Dialogue and Lyrics, 1982

Ek Pal, Screenplay, Dialogue and Lyrics, 1983

Sadma, Screenplay, Dialogue and Lyrics, 1983

Ghulami, Lyrics, 1987

Maya Memsaab, Lyrics, 1993

Swami Vivekanand, Lyrics, 1994

Rudaali, Screenplay, Dialogue and Lyrics, 1995

Mammo, Lyrics, 1995

Aastha, Lyrics, 1997

Daayra, Lyrics, 1997

Chachi 420, Dialogue and Lyrics, 1997

Satya, Lyrics, 1998

Dil Se…, Lyrics, 1998

Fiza, Lyrics, 2000

Aks, Lyrics, 2001

Ashoka the Great, Lyrics, 2001

Filhaal…, Lyrics, 2002

Laal Salaam, Lyrics, 2002

Leela, Lyrics, 2002

Saathiya, Dialogue and Lyrics, 2002

Makdee, Lyrics, 2003

Pinjar, Lyrics, 2003

Maqbool, Lyrics, 2004

Chupke Se, Lyrics, 2004

Raincoat, Lyrics, 2004

Bunty aur Babli, Lyrics, 2005

Paheli, Lyrics, 2005

Yahaan, Lyrics, 2005

Omkaara, Lyrics, 2006

Jaan-e-Mann, Lyrics, 2006

Dus Kahaniyaan, Screenplay and Dialogue – 'Gubbare', 2007

The Blue Umbrella, Lyrics, 2007

Guru, Lyrics, 2007

Jhoom Barabar Jhoom, Lyrics, 2007

Just Married, Lyrics, 2007

No Smoking, Lyrics, 2007

Dum Kata, Lyrics, 2007

Yuvraaj, Lyrics, 2008

Slumdog Millionaire, Lyrics, 2008

Billu, Lyrics, 2009

Firaaq, Lyrics, 2009

Kaminey, Lyrics, 2009

Dus Tola, Lyrics, 2010

Raajneeti, Lyrics, 2010

Veer, Lyrics, 2010

Ishqiya, Lyrics, 2010

Striker, Lyrics, 2010

Raavan, Lyrics, 2010

7 Khoon Maaf, Lyrics, 2011

Kashmakash, Lyrics, 2011

Teen Thay Bhai, Lyrics, 2011

Chala Mussaddi … Office Office, Lyrics, 2011

Jab Tak Hai Jaan, Lyrics, 2012

Do Paise Ki Dhoop, Chaar Aane Ki Baarish, Lyrics, 2012

Matru Ki Bijli Ka Mandola, Lyrics, 2013

Ek Thi Daayan, Lyrics, 2013

Kya Dilli Kya Lahore, Lyrics, 2014

Dedh Ishqiya, Lyrics, 2014

Haider, Lyrics, 2014

Kill Dill, Lyrics, 2014

Lingaa, Lyrics, 2014

Drishyam, Lyrics, 2015

Talvar, Lyrics, 2015

Mirzya, Screenplay, Dialogue and Lyrics, 2016

Ok Jaanu, Lyrics, 2017

Rangoon, Lyrics, 2017

Raazi, Lyrics, 2018

Soorma, Lyrics, 2018

Awards...

2003 Sahitya Akademi Award for *Dhuaan* (Urdu short stories)

2004 Padma Bhushan

2008 Academy Award for Best Original Song as Lyricist for
'Jai Ho' (Slumdog Millionaire). Shared with A.R. Rahman

2010 Grammy Award for Best Song Written for a Motion Picture,
Television or Other Visual Media for *Jai Ho' (Slumdog Millionaire)*.
Shared with A.R. Rahman and Tanvi Shah

2012 Indira Gandhi Award for National Integration

2013 Dadasaheb Phalke Award – the highest award in Indian cinema

Honorary Awards

2001 Lifetime Honorary Fellowship from the Indian Institute of Advanced
Studies, Simla

2009 Honorary Doctorate from Punjab University, Patiala

2012 Honorary Doctorate in Urdu Literature – Maulana Azad National
University, Hyderabad

2013 Appointed Hon. Chancellor, Sikkim University

2014 Honorary Doctoratefrom University of Hyderabad

2015 Doctor of Letters from Rabindra Bharati University, Kolkata

Filmfare Awards

1971 Best Dialogue *Anand*

1973 Best Dialogue *Namak Haram*

1975 Best Feature Film (Critics) *Aandhi*

1976 Best Director *Mausam*

1977 Best Lyricist *'Do diwaane shahar mein'* (*Gharonda*)

1979 Best Lyricist *'Aanewala pal jaane wala hai'* (*Gol Maal*)

1980 Best Lyricist *'Hazaar raahen mud ke dekhin'* (*Thodi Si Bewafaai*)

1983 Best Lyricist *'Tujhse naraaz nahin zindagi'* (*Masoom*)

1988 Best Lyricist *'Mera kuchh saamaan'* (*Ijaazat*)

1991 Best Lyricist *'Yaara seeli seeli'* (*Lekin…*)

1991 Best Documentary *Ustad Amjad Ali Khan*

1996 Best Dialogue *Maachis*

1996 Best Story, *Maachis*

1998 Best Lyricist *'Chhaiyya chhaiyya…'* (*Dil Se…*)

2002 Lifetime Achievement Award

2003 Best Lyricist *'Saathiya…'* (*Saathiya*)

2003 Best Dialogue *Saathiya*

2006 Best Lyricist *'Kajra re'* (*Bunty aur Babli*)

2011 Best Lyricist *'Dil toh bachcha hai ji'* (*Ishqiya*)

2013 Best Lyricist *'Chhalla…'* (*Jab Tak Hai Jaan*)

National Awards

1972 Best Screenplay *Koshish*

1976 Best Director *Mausam*

1998 Best Lyricist '*Mera kuchh saaman*' (*Ijaazat*)

1991 Best Lyricist '*Yaara seeli seeli*' (*Lekin…*)

1991 Best Documentary *Ustad Amjad Ali Khan*

1993 Best Documentary *Pandit Bhimsen Joshi*

1996 Best Film Providing Wholesome Entertainment *Maachis*

Index